GARTH TURNER'S

2001

RETIREMENT
GUIDE

HOW TO BUILD
YOUR WEALTH AND
RETIRE IN
COMFORT

KEY PORTER BOOKS

Canadian Cataloguing in Publication Data

The National Library of Canada has catalogued this publication as follows:

Turner, Garth
    Garth Turner's 2001 Retirement Guide

Annual.
1997-
ISSN: 1482-003X
ISBN: 1-55263-296-2 (2001)

1. Registered Retirement Savings Plans. 2. Tax shelters – Canada.   I. Title.

HD7129.T87   332.6'042   C97-301886-0

The Canada Council Le Conseil des Arts
for the arts du Canada
since 1957 depuis 1957

The publisher gratefully acknowledges the support of the Canada Council for the Arts and the Ontario Arts Council for its publishing program.

We acknowledge the financial support of the Government of Canada through the Book Publishing Industry Development Program (BPIDP) for our publishing activities.

Key Porter Books Limited
70 The Esplanade
Toronto, Ontario
Canada M5E 1R2

www.keyporter.com

Electronic formatting: Heidi Palfrey
Design: Peter Maher

Printed and bound in Canada

01 02 03 6 5 4 3 2

Contents

2001: A Retirement Odyssey

BEFORE YOU BEGIN

Welcome to the lean and mean version of my annual RRSP and retirement guide. Regular readers will notice that this edition is half the size of the previous one.

Since we are all short of time, and 250 pages of text is a lot to digest, I have reduced this Guide to a more reasonable size, stripping away the excess and giving you more tips and easy-to-implement lists. You will be able to read this in a couple of hours, and then get on with the huge task of preparing for a secure retirement.

Additional material is contained in the CD-ROM that is included with this volume. For the first time in Canadian history, original audio and video programming has been created for a book—a television-like guide to retirement planning strategies that you can watch on your computer. It takes about 40 minutes to view, and you get the basic choices for your courses of action.

You can also visit me on the Internet and use the retirement calculator that will give you an instant snapshot of whether you are on the right path and, if not, how to get there. The address: *www.garthRRSPguide.com.* Go there and spend a few minutes filling out the personalized form. The information will be kept completely confidential and private, and will enable me to get back to you with some practical solutions for your own situation.

This Guide, then, sets out to help you achieve financial goals that, unfortunately, most of your friends, coworkers and neighbours will never attain. Most Canadians are in rotten shape when it comes to their money, because they have blown a few basic decisions.

The good news is that, if my predictions are correct, the next few years will provide a once-in-a-lifetime opportunity of reversing that trend. A booming economy and roaring financial markets will afford us all the chance of building wealth and preparing for a much harsher decade that follows this one. But there is no time to lose.

For aging baby boomers like me, this Guide is critical stuff. Entering our fifties, we now have just over a decade to do some amazing things—get rid of the mortgage, shift more wealth into financial assets, earn double-digit rates of return, employ expert financial help, defer taxation, get the right insurance strategies and plan for a retirement that could last 30 to 40 years. With the proper attention, all of these things can be done, but there is not a day to lose.

The stakes are also high for people in their thirties and forties. Those boomers will be a social drag for decades to come, tipping the economy into a negative spin by about 2015. The next decade is when personal assets must be built quickly. This is no time for caution and conservatism, but rather for a lusty investment strategy that sees you embrace the new technologies and harness the momentum of rapidly rising markets. Common sense and long-term vision are your weapons against inevitable bouts of temporary volatility. Have courage, and take charge.

Those in their twenties or younger should realize that the bulk of their life will be turbulent. They are coming of age within one of the most profound technological revolutions in history. The very nature of human interaction is changing. When their parents were their age, television was a novelty and computers were unknown. (Hey, when my father was a kid there were still stagecoaches in Ontario!) The next quarter century will accelerate the pace of that change, extending human life by up to 30%, drawing the world into one giant economy, erasing national currencies such as the Canadian dollar, sucking the value out of some entire industries (such as newsprint and oil) and blowing it directly into others (such as biotechnology), while also bringing us to the verge of ecological collapse.

Given all of this intense change, you should be establishing financial goals today, and working towards them. There is no instrument more useful, flexible or potent than the RRSP in achieving those goals.

I say this knowing full well that a trendy school of thought has developed among many young people that RRSPs are passé, pedestrian and fodder for a major tax hit later in life. The reality is that money multiplies faster in the tax-free environment of an RRSP than anywhere else. In addition, you get immediate tax relief for contributing to your plan. And using the right strategies, it is possible to remove money from your retirement plan later and actually pay little or no tax on it. This Guide will show you how.

I will also show you how to get 100% foreign content in your RRSP and avoid our ailing loonie; how to make RRSP contributions even when you have no cash; and how to exceed the government's own RRSP contribution rules. You can seize your mortgage and put it inside your RRSP, making mortgage payments to yourself. You can take assets and investments you already own, and make them tax-free. You can use an RRSP to inflate the down payment on a home, or remove money from your RRIF and pay no tax on it.

In short, you have an incredible tool here. Those who choose to use it fully can construct a financial future that is both worry-free and rewarding. Those who do not will likely run out of money. It will not be a happy time 25 years from now when millions of people are in the same boat. Already, it seems, many of us suspect what is coming.

Just a few years ago, a plan called "Freedom 55" sparked the imagination of many middle-aged people who wanted to call it quits at age 55. Today it could be more like "Freedom 85," according to a recent survey conducted by the American Association of Retired Persons. The poll, taken by Roper Starch Worldwide Inc., found that the overwhelming majority (80%) of baby boomers today expect to continue working in their "retirement years," which effectively means no retirement until you are unable to work anymore.

I don't know about you, but I do not intend this picture to include me. Some media critics have called me aggressive, which is probably true, but anyone who is determined to achieve, and maintain, financial security must break with the herd. Sadly, that herd has been badly informed.

Example: A year ago, as I was writing the 2000 version of this Guide, people were being whipped into a frenzy of paralysis by pundits who warned that financial markets would crash and that stock and mutual fund investors be destroyed by the chaos of Y2K.

Partially as a result of this fabricated scaremongering, Canadian investors retreated into a shell, shunning mutual funds, ploughing money into GICs and money market funds and ignoring the huge opportunities posed by market volatility as the millennium dawned. Far from melting down, the stock market in 2000 surged higher on a tide of sound economic news and technological advance—just as last year's version of this Guide forecast.

Consider the facts, instead of the hype, and then decide whether you want to be a saver or an investor (and there is a huge difference between the two). In 2000:

- The Toronto stock market hit the highest point ever—again, and again, and again. Within seven months of Y2K it had advanced by more than 25%.
- Despite a wild (and temporary) surge in the world price of crude oil, core inflation in Canada barely budged over 1%, setting the stage for sustained economic growth.
- Taxes came down, in both provincial and federal budgets. Ottawa gave stock and fund investors a direct gift by slicing the capital gains tax rate; and this is only a taste of what lies ahead.
- The human genome project succeeded in mapping DNA—the building block of the human body, paving the way for a massive move forward that could see the end of ailments such as cancer and Alzheimer's disease within the decade.
- Corporate profits surged. The banks recorded their best year ever. For the first time in five years the TSE 300 surpassed the Dow in New York.
- The Canadian Venture Exchange exploded higher.
- Unemployment dropped to a 19-year low.
- Economists were universal in their predictions of booming years to come.
- More than 800 mutual funds available to Canadians gave a one-year return in excess of 20%. This occurred at the same time as GICs were paying 5% and residential real estate in Toronto, one of the country's hottest markets, was enjoying a gain barely equalling inflation.

These things are not flukes. They are not temporary. Instead they are harbingers of what you can expect to come over the next decade. They are exactly what I predicted would occur in my 1995 book, *2015: After the Boom* and I am revoicing my convictions yet again. We are on the verge of the best economic years in the lives of most people. You should expect the TSE 300 to achieve 20,000 within in the next five to seven years—roughly twice its current value. Well-managed equity mutual funds will provide annual yields of 10% to 20%. Good science and technology funds will at least double that return.

Interest rates will be lower in a year than they are today and I expect we will have seen at least one major bank merger take place. Taxes will continue to fall, along with the unemployment rate—both major stimulants to economic growth.

These are ideal conditions for RRSP investors who make aggressive use of the strategies this Guide contains. And for those who choose not to act, by contrast, the years ahead will be most difficult. By 2015, half the population will be over the age of 40, for the first time. By 2030 the number of retired people will have mushroomed, with over eight million 70-year-olds.

Imagine what that will do to the health care system and the public pension plan.

Right now about half of Canadians have no retirement savings and the half who do have an average RRSP of $40,000, which is growing by $4,000 a year. At that rate today's 50-year-old boomer will have about $100,000 by age 65. I calculate that is 10% of what that person will need to finance another 20 years.

Last year fewer than one in ten people contributing to an RRSP made the maximum amount while about five in ten were watching *Who Wants to Be a Millionaire?*

So, turn off the TV and pop in my CD. Read this book, or any other RRSP guide on the shelf. Do just one thing this week to get ahead— arrange for a monthly RRSP contribution, or borrow money to catch up on missed payments, or cash in a GIC and buy a mutual fund, or seek out a financial adviser. Break from the herd. Focus on the incredibly positive and bright few years ahead and—whatever happens—do not squander them or be diverted from your path by the doubters and the timid who surround us.

They are not worthy of preventing you and your family from finding financial freedom. Let's go.

Chapter 1

Changes for 2001:
A grudging hand

Now that we've got the first year of the new millennium under our belts, things don't look so bad. Of course, there are those purists who insist the new millennium does not kick in until 2001. But let's face it, sticking a 20 in front of the year's date instead of 19 seemed good cause for a celebration.

First and foremost, Y2K became the peril that never was. But much more appreciable was the way the TSE rocketed from the 7,000+ level to catch the Dow and kiss the 11,000 mark.

And to cap things off, the federal government grudgingly tossed us a bone—lower taxes (a bit now, some more later), plus a small boost to RRSP investors. It's about time. Personal income taxes are now beginning to fall, the dreaded bracket-creep factor has finally been dispatched, and you can use that extra cash to take advantage of higher limits on RRSP foreign content.

For the tax year 2000, you are allowed up to 25% foreign content in your RRSP. That will jump further for the 2001 tax year, up to 30%. And with about 97% of the world's financial capitalization located outside Canada, it couldn't come at a better time.

The only other small change of note is that you can now bequeath your RRSP to the charity of your choice. You just have to write the name of the charity in the beneficiary spot and that's that. Prior to this, you had to name the estate as beneficiary and the donation would come from the estate, after the feds took their share of the collapsed RRSP.

RECAP: BUDGETS PAST

The government roughed up the RRSP rules in the 1996 budget, but little has changed since then. For those who missed highlights of RRSP rule changes in past years, the following should bring you up to speed:

BUDGET 1999

The most significant aspect of this budget is that one of the worst-conceived pieces of legislation, the proposed Seniors Benefit, was scrapped. The government never managed to sell the benign-sounding Seniors Benefit to the Canadian population at large. Some low-income Canadians would have received a modest increase under the plan; however, the program was poised to take billions of dollars in extra tax from middle-class, middle-income retirees based on their family income, not their individual income.

Benign, it certainly wasn't. And Canada's gray power demographic let the government know that. And let's face it, seniors can be a feisty lot. Even Finance Minister Paul Martin eventually admitted that the proposed legislation was seriously flawed. Good riddance.

Education and your RRSP

There were only two other RRSP items to consider: one was a program that allows you or your spouse to withdraw RRSP funds to pursue additional education. You can now withdraw, tax-free, up to $10,000 a year over a four-year period to a maximum withdrawal of $20,000.

You must repay the money in equal annual installments within 10 years, starting in the year following the last year you were enrolled as a student. If your studies end in 2001, then payback begins in 2002. However, repayment must begin no later than the sixth year after the initial withdrawal. Slower learners take heed.

The danger with this program, as with the Home Buyers' Plan, is that money withdrawn for a period of time means you're losing years of tax-free compounding. So if you can find financing somewhere else, do it.

The other item of note was the introduction of a grant program— the Canada Education Savings Grant (CESG)—with which the government will boost Registered Education Savings Plan (RESP) contributions.

On the first $2,000 contributed for each child under the age of 19, the government will add 20% directly to the RESP. An annual $2,000 contribution will see the plan receive a $400 boost from the feds. Talk to your financial adviser about these plans. They are now more flexible than before, and the CESG will add to that allure. No tax refund for a contribution, but the money in the RESP can grow unfettered by taxes.

Source: Toronto Sun

NEW AND DIFFERENT IN 1998

Changes were few and far between. In fact, there was just one major change: the restoration of lost RRSP room for individuals who leave a job and take with them a lump-sum payout from a company pension plan. Of course, you wouldn't take such a payout in a cheque (tax hit), but would instead arrange to roll it over into your personal RRSP (see Chapter 12).

OTHER MEMORABLE TWEAKING

The 1995 budget scaled back the maximum contribution level by $1,000 to $13,500 until the end of 1997. But the 1997 budget drastically extended that freeze, which will mean that people earning over $75,000 a year will pay more tax and contribute less to their plans.

The RRSP dollar limit is now frozen until 2003, although there was some talk after the last election of raising it by year 2000. Too late for that now. After that it is scheduled to rise to $14,500 in 2004 and then to $15,500 in 2005—a whole decade later than that level was supposed to have been achieved.

Following this, contribution limits will be indexed to the average wage, which has been barely moving higher through most of the past decade.

No more carry-forward limit

This was good news of a sort. Since 1991, you have been allowed to carry forward RRSP contributions that you didn't, or couldn't, make for seven years. This is a great idea, and a real blessing to people who have had a tough financial time over the last few years. The seven-year limit on carrying forward those missed contributions has been eliminated—for now, at least.

While this is an improvement, it also poses a danger. If people know they can catch up later, they may be inclined to spend their money now on a better lifestyle in the knowledge that no contribution room is being lost. And that would be a huge mistake.

Administration fees no longer tax-deductible

The annual administrative fee to run a self-directed plan is no longer deductible from your taxes when paid outside the plan. This fee is typically about $150 a year. But as explained in the section on self-directed RRSPs, deductible fee or not, you must have one of these plans.

In a post-budget interpretation, Canada Customs and Revenue Agency stated that RRSP or RRIF administration fees paid outside the account will be considered a contribution to the RRSP, while fees paid inside will be considered a taxable withdrawal.

Counselling fees also not deductible

Here was a real sleeper—contained in a single paragraph buried in a technical "Notice of Ways and Means Motion" portion of the 1997 budget. And while it does not affect many people, those who are affected will take a significant tax whack. The money that wealthier people pay to have their RRSPs or RRIFs managed is no longer considered a deductible expense.

This change will come to have a much greater significance in later years as baby boomers amass the capital they will need to retire with a half-decent income. Somebody today in their mid-thirties, making maximum RRSP contributions for the next 30 years, will easily have a million-dollar investment to manage.

And as more high-income earners today are downsized with large locked-in RRSPs that will grow over the years, they, too, will be hit with this tax that Ottawa tried so hard to hide in the back of the budget book.

No more retiring allowance

This was a stinker. A retirement allowance is money you receive when you retire, quit or are laid off. Up until the 1995 budget, you could roll over a big chunk of this cash directly into your RRSP. This is being phased out—and it's a real crime. You can read the details in Chapter 12.

Two fewer years to contribute

This was a big change. The length of time you can contribute money into an RRSP has been reduced by two years. At a certain point in your life, the rules say you must stop putting away money for your old age, and start withdrawing it—and the best way of doing that is to convert the RRSP into a RRIF (more on that later). That age had been 71, and now it's 69.

This change is significant for many reasons. Obviously, it will put more money into Ottawa's coffers as two years of tax deferral are swept away. This one change means we have all potentially lost $31,000 in tax-deductible savings.

Some of these recent changes are indeed daunting. But do not let any of this deter you—the changes simply underscore the need to take maximum advantage of the remaining opportunities. Your RRSP is still an awesome personal finance vehicle.

Think about it. . .

. . .over the past 40 years the TSE 300 has had five years of double-digit drops. But more importantly, it has had 22 years of double-digit gains.

REMEMBER:

- Your RRSP is the best foundation of your entire investment program.
- The more the benefits are reduced, the more aggressive you must become.
- Maximize annual contributions and contribute early in the tax year—it can provide tens of thousands of dollars in extra assets.
- Can't find a lump sum to contribute? Then set up a monthly pre-authorized contribution and enjoy reduced taxes on your paycheque.
- Borrow the money. Most banks, trusts, credit unions and many brokers or planners will lend you money at prime, or cheaper. Use the tax refund to pay down the loan.

"What, me worry?"

Why you should and why you shouldn't

Since the meltdown of the civilized world failed to materialize as the calendar and clocks turned over to January 1, 2000 (much to the chagrin of many so-called pundits), Canada's economy has continued to motor along unimpeded. Corporate profits are improving. Interest rates are manageable. The Toronto Stock Exchange is in a neck-and-neck race with the Dow—it's already bouncing around the 11,000 mark and could well crack 12,000 or higher in 2001. Core inflation is steady, oil prices aside. Consumer confidence is far from waning. And employers continue to scramble to find enough workers.

When you consider the economic fundamentals in play, most of them add up to good times ahead. Then why should any of us worry?

Well, for starters, over the next three decades, almost 10 million Canadians will retire. Consider these numbers:

- In the last 25 years the number of seniors has doubled.
- The fastest-growing age category over the next four years will be 45- to 54-year-olds.
- The fastest-growing age group over the next 20 years will be people over age 80.

This means:

- The cost of health care will soar, by at least 50%.
- Most residential real estate will likely see its value erode.
- Government medical/pension benefits could increase taxes on working Canadians.

A few years back, in a chilling report entitled "Beyond the Deficit: Generation X and Sustainable Debt," the C.D. Howe Institute stated the obvious: today's relatively well-off middle-aged and middle-class taxpayers will have to shoulder more of a burden. To do that, urged McMaster University economist William Scarth, government must, among other things:

- Toughen up pension rules for the wealthy
- Impose user fees
- End the universality of social programs

That is clearly the direction the federal government must head. But more tax on the wealthy is not enough. Scarth argues that the future will be bleak even with Ottawa balancing its budget, and that the feds must run a surplus for the next decade, and vastly reduce the level of federal debt to meet the coming retirement crunch. Are your finances ready?

Action Plan Requirement. . .

Maximize RRSPs now—sheltering income from an increasing tax load, harnessing the power of rising financial markets and building a defence against what could be a desperate time beyond 2015.

Proportionate to the size of our population, Canada has the biggest baby-boom generation in the world. That means it will also likely have the biggest retirement crisis in the world. Our relatively small population means Canada's prosperity is overly dependent on trade. But our main trading partners also have aging populations, and face similar domestic problems—specifically caring for the health of a rapidly aging population.

Consider this. . .

Up to 90% of a person's total lifetime medical costs can be incurred in the last six months of life.

Future costs of our current medical system are "unaffordable." Caring for today's population will cost today's taxpayers $1 trillion.

"In the short run, the earning power of the baby boomers will go a long way towards supporting existing spending patterns," according to a report on health care by the Canadian Institute of Actuaries.

"However, just after the turn of the century, the situation will change significantly. The leading edge of the age bulge reaches 55 in the year 2000, and will begin to retire. That will have the two-edged effect that the productive base will begin to shrink and the high health care-user group will expand."

Source: David Brown, Toronto Star

If nothing is done, each worker in 2031 will have to produce 60% more than he or she did in 1991 to care for senior dependants. That, as you can well imagine, is totally impossible.

Did you know. . .

. . .that for a 45-year-old man to purchase long-term care insurance for his declining years, he would have to pay about $163 a month for 20 years? That would provide up to $200 a day of long-term care at home or in a facility. But William M. Mercer Ltd. benefits consultant Malcolm Hamilton says that while $200 may seem like a lot today, in 30 years it may not even get you in the door of a long-term care institution.

As longevity continues to increase, today's boomers will be paying more for the health care of their aging parents. Tomorrow, Generation X will be faced with a stunning health bill to fund the hip replacements and pacemakers of legions of retired baby boomers.

Today the estimated health care bill for people over age 65 for the rest of their lives is $369 billion. But the health bill for all the people who are working today, over the course of their lives, is $1 trillion—most of it payable in about 30 years. Make no mistake about it: this scenario will make a huge dent in Canada's standard of living.

A fact of life. . .

With life expectancies far greater than most men, women must be even more concerned and proactive in their attempts to provide for their later years. Yet many, if not most, are not taking any action now to ensure that they are not marginalized as they join the ranks of the elderly.

Yes, it's time to worry. Most Canadians, both men and women, are ignoring the issue. Dealing with it should be at the top of the national political agenda. The fact that it is not a top priority pretty much guarantees a dark future for the unprepared.

Retirement financing for today's boomers will be tough enough. For people in their twenties and thirties, it will be a nightmare unless drastic change occurs.

According to the Institute for Research on Public Policy, correcting the intergenerational imbalance would mean:

* Gutting today's benefits for seniors—ripe for a revolt
* Permanently raising taxes each year by 1.2%—revolting, but not out of the question
* Cutting government purchases by 10.4%—a revolutionary idea, but what are the odds of it happening?

Without that kind of action, this is how the tax and benefit scorecard looks:

Age and sex now	Get more in benefits	Pay more in taxes
Newborn boy		$131,200
Newborn girl		$56,700
25-year-old man		$290,000
25-year-old woman		$136,000
65-year-old man	$121,400	
65-year-old woman	$108,100	

A person born in 1911, for example, will get a 22.4% return on the money he paid out in Canada Pension Plan contributions. A person born today will get a rate of return of about 1.5% on all the money she'll pay in during a whole lifetime. As the actuaries pointed out in their report on the future of the public pension plan, it was "enacted in 1965, when Canada was nearing the end of an unprecedented 20-year economic boom. The economy had grown quickly in real terms. Interest rates, nominal and real, were low.

"Ironically, the great baby boom ended about 18 months after the Canada Pension Plan was created—with its whole funding premise that the babies would never stop coming."

As a matter of fact. . .

. . .asking Canadians for an extra 70% in premiums may not do the trick, says Lloyd Atkinson of Perigee Investment Counsel Inc. He warns that the retirement age might have to be increased to 67, and benefits clawed back even more than expected, and that further down the road the retirement age could again be raised higher.

It's unlikely that the CPP will not stay afloat. But your retirement planning should include no allowance for public pension income. Yes, financial markets will rise and the economy will improve for at least a decade, maybe more. But beyond that, things become a lot murkier—especially for most people who are unprepared for what we know is coming.

Based on current evidence:

- Taxes will likely increase in the future, not decrease
- The level of government support will fall
- Most of today's middle-aged, middle-class people will receive no public pensions
- There will be a health care crisis as long as we try to maintain a universal, public, free-access system

Faced with millions more elderly people, care will either have to be rationed or the system at least partially privatized. Either way, it will cost a lot more to get sick in 2020 than it does today.

Now that you're worried, here's the good news

RRSP investors today are presented with wonderful, almost unparalleled, opportunities to make their money grow. Here are some factors:

- The aging population means lower inflation that will also knock down interest rates over the long term.
- The value of real assets—real estate, gold, Porsches—will decline, but financial asset values will rise.
- Quality stocks, bonds and mutual funds will catapult higher as money flows out of real assets.

Combined with this is the fact that the baby-boom generation is entering its peak earning and spending years. Many people in this age group have the mortgage paid off, giving them more disposable income. And as they start hitting age 50 at the same time, they will do to stocks, bonds and funds what they did to real estate in the 1980s— drive valuations higher.

If you know that now, in 2001, then I think you know where to invest. And you know where not to invest.

Don't worry, do this

As shocking a notion as this might seem, here's what you must do. If you are middle aged or older, systematically remove equity from residential real estate and transfer it to financial assets. This means:

- You don't have to sell your home; just borrow against your paid-up house
- Sell your home if it's time to downsize; now is as good a time as any
- Channel the money into assets such as equities and mutual funds

Canadians have 70% of their net worth in residential real estate— which is far too much. Besides, most residential real estate faces a bleak long-term future.

Meanwhile, equity-based mutual funds that track stock market performance have been growing by double digits. These booming financial markets will continue to make tracks upward. For people who are serious about growing their wealth, the timing could hardly be better to be buying equity funds, stocks, or indexed or exchange-traded funds.

Worried about the future? Good, that's the first step. The second step? Commit to taking action now, and put those worries behind you. Step three? There is no easier way to accomplish this than within an RRSP. Here's how. . . .

Chapter 3

What you must know and remember

Two-thirds of Canadians don't have an RRSP. Many have no idea what an RRSP is, nor do they realize how one could improve their financial lot.

I should be surprised at this, but I'm not. After all, this isn't taught in schools, and most companies handling RRSPs do little to inform and educate the masses in a concise, straightforward manner. The complexities and ramifications of an RRSP can boggle the mind. But it doesn't have to be a total mystery.

THE STRUCTURE

Imagine a large bubble where you can encapsulate your financial assets—shielded from taxes—allowing them to grow and compound. That bubble is an RRSP. It is not a product that you buy at the bank. An RRSP is not a thing—it's a process.

As a matter of fact. . .

. . .50% of Canadians claim to have a financial adviser, yet only one-third of these individuals actually have a financial plan for retirement. So says a survey conducted by A.C. Nielsen on behalf of the Canadian Imperial Bank of Commerce. The poll also discovered that 80% of those aged 18 to 35 have no plan at all.

Still, only five million of us have started saving using this wonderful tool. The rest are paying more taxes than necessary, on investments that all too often provide insufficient returns.

A FEW BASICS

A Registered Retirement Savings Plan (RRSP) lets you:

- Defer taxes on money you save today
- Pay those taxes in retirement when you are in a lower tax bracket

The benefits of opening an RRSP and contributing to it every month or year are enormous:

- Money put in the plan is deducted from your taxable income, meaning a big tax refund cheque.
- Taxable investments can be put in your RRSP, and will grow in value tax-free.
- On retirement you can roll your RRSP assets over into a RRIF (Registered Retirement Income Fund), which further defers taxes as long as you withdraw a minimal amount from the plan every year.
- You can save a bundle on lifetime taxes.
- You can use an RRSP to split income with your less-taxed spouse.

Simply put: This is the best leg-up on the future that you're likely to get.

WHO CAN CONTRIBUTE?

If you earn income, you can contribute to an RRSP until the end of the year in which you turn 69. If you turn 70 in 2002, then you have until December 31, 2001, to contribute to your plan. Then you should convert it into an RRIF and start withdrawing money. You can also continue putting money into your spouse's RRSP, regardless of your age, until that spouse turns 69. There is no minimum age—as long as you earn income. You should, however, file a tax return, even in years when no taxes are due.

HOW MUCH CAN YOU CONTRIBUTE?

That depends on your income. If you work for a company that has a pension plan, your maximum contribution for the 2000 tax year is 18% of your 1999 income, minus a pension adjustment—to a maximum of $13,500.

For those without a company plan, the limit is 18% of income to a maximum of $13,500. To reach that level, your income must be $75,000, putting you in the top 6% of Canadian earners.

WHAT IF I MISS A YEAR?

You can catch up on missed contributions, but you can never catch up on the tax-free financial assets that those contributions could have earned during the time you did not make your contribution.

WHAT IF I OVERCONTRIBUTE?

You can overcontribute without penalty, as long as it doesn't exceed $2,000 during your lifetime. There's no tax deduction for an overcontribution, but it can still grow tax-free within your plan. And you can use it in future years for future RRSP payments. Overcontributions can be withdrawn, but in most cases you will be charged withholding tax, which you claim back on your income tax return by filing Form 3012A.

If you exceed the $2,000 limit, Canada Customs and Revenue Agency (formerly Revenue Canada) will box your ears, charging you a penalty of 1% a month on the extra until it is removed. Children under age 18 at the beginning of the year can't make the overcontribution. They can do so the year following the year in which they turn 19.

WHEN CAN YOU CONTRIBUTE?

Many people think they can only make a contribution in January or February 2001—the "RRSP season" for the 2000 year. But you could have started loading up your 2000 contribution back in January 2000—a full 14 months before the 2000 contribution deadline of February 28, 2001.

You should make every effort to contribute as early as possible for the current tax year, not the previous one. This means that your money compounds for an extra year, and you could be tens of thousands of dollars ahead in retirement. Now, if it's hard to find a big pile of extra money each year, contribute monthly—and see your paycheque taxes reduced.

Consider this. . .

If you are 32 years old and put $4,300 into your RRSP every year until age 65—and it earns an average of 8%—you'll have more than $600,000 on retirement. If you start doing this at age 20, by 65 you can have more than twice that amount—about $1.5 million.

WHAT'S THE TAX BREAK?

The more money you make, the bigger the break. The entire contribution amount is deducted from your taxable income. If you contribute $5,000 and you are in the 40% tax bracket, you save $2,000; in the 54% tax bracket, you save $2,700.

WHAT CAN GO IN MY BUBBLE?

A huge number of financial assets can go into an RRSP, but most people—wrongly—put their retirement savings into GICs or savings bonds. Other things you can put in your RRSP include:

• Mutual funds, segregated funds or exchange-traded funds
• Term deposits
• Canadian stocks
• Corporate strip bonds
• Federal and provincial government bonds
• Crown corporation bonds
• Foreign government bonds
• Limited partnership units
• Labour-sponsored venture capital funds
• Small business shares
• Mortgages
• Your own mortgage

WHAT CAN'T BE IN MY RRSP?

Real estate, precious metals, foreign currency, art, antiques, put options, commodities or futures. But existing rules allow you to put real estate or gold mutual funds or stocks in your RRSP, as well as bonds or other securities denominated in foreign currencies.

HOW MANY PLANS CAN I HAVE?

As many as you want—even several RRSPs at several financial institutions. This is not recommended, though. Each plan—if it's self-directed (and it should be) costs about $150 a year to administer, but that fee is not tax-deductible. In addition, there are often transaction fees and it's sometimes hard to manage multiple plans.

My advice? Just have one, big, self-directed plan—managed by a smart financial adviser—and invested in equity mutual funds, stocks, federal and provincial government bonds, Crown corporation bonds and corporate bonds. Costs are kept in check, and it's easy to measure monthly performance.

CAN I BORROW FOR MY RRSP?

Yes, but the interest is not tax-deductible. But that doesn't mean you should not borrow to make the annual maximum allowable contribution. Here's why:

• Most financial institutions will give you an RRSP loan at their best rate—usually prime. Many brokerages or financial planning firms will even get you money below the prime rate, as long as they are managing your portfolio.
• An RRSP contribution will net you a tax refund. Just take that refund back to where you borrowed the money and use it to pay down a major part of that loan.
• Astute investing in conservatively managed, equity-based mutual funds will earn tax-free returns well in excess of the cost of borrowing.
• If you can pay off the loan within a year—by the time you need another one—you're doing just fine.

Here is an example of why it's smart to borrow so you can make your maximum annual RRSP contribution. Let's say you have $5,000 to invest, but under the rules you could put in $10,000. How much further ahead would you be by borrowing the other $5,000?

	Invest $5,000	Invest $10,000 (with a loan)
Tax refund at 40% rate	$2,000	$4,000
Invest in a security		
yielding 7%	350	700
You're ahead by this much	$2,350	$ 4,700
Use refund to pay down loan		−4,000
Repay rest of loan at 7%		−1,070
Net gain	$2,000	−1,070
RRSP assets	$5,350	$10,700
Total assets	$7,350	$ 9,630

A fact of life. . .

London Life Insurance estimates that a couple can currently have a comfortable retirement on an annual after-tax income of $20,350. For an above-average retirement, a couple will need $37,000 a year in after-tax income, while $81,400 annually can deliver a luxurious lifestyle.

DO I NEED FOREIGN CONTENT?

Smart people know not to have all their eggs in one basket—or all your wealth in Canadian dollars. The rules allow you to have up to 25% of the total book value of your RRSP in foreign securities. For the 2001 tax year and thereafter it will be 30%. There are also many more funds now coming into the market offering foreign content but that are 100% RRSP eligible. Check them out with your adviser.

CAN MY RRSP HELP BUY A HOUSE?

Under the Home Buyers' Plan, first-time buyers can withdraw up to $20,000 for a down payment or, together with your spouse, up to $40,000. The money must be paid back into your RRSP, but you get 15 years to do that. This is the only way I know of getting $40,000 tax-free and interest-free. But remember, money withdrawn from your RRSP is no longer compounding tax-free.

CAN I SPLIT INCOME WITH AN RRSP?

Absolutely. You do not want to end up in retirement with the bulk of your family assets in the name of the person who pays the most tax— but that is what happens to most Canadians.

Typically, the husband makes the most money, makes the most investments and ends up in the top marginal tax bracket. That family could vastly improve its income level and standard of living by simply shifting assets into the name of the lower-taxed spouse.

You're allowed to contribute to your husband or wife's RRSP, up to the same level you could put money into your own plan. After a short period, those assets then belong to the other person and when cashed in, are taxed at his or her rate, not yours.

CAN I TRANSFER BETWEEN PLANS?

Canada Customs and Revenue Agency (CCRA) imposes no penalties for transfers, but switches can often be a real hassle because financial institutions get cranky about sending money to other institutions. Expect to pay a fee to the bank or trust, and expect delays. Ensure that the bank has the paperwork long before the switch will occur.

TIP: The company you are transferring your RRSP to will be happy for the business—probably happy enough to pay the fee from the transferring company. Be sure to ask about it before committing.

WHAT HAPPENS IF I DON'T LIVE FOREVER?

This is Canada—when you die, you pay tax. Upon death an RRSP is deemed cashed out, and your estate pays big bucks in tax because the whole amount is added to your taxable income that year.

For this reason, you should not write "Estate" on the RRSP application that asks you who should be the beneficiary. You can roll over your entire RRSP assets, free of tax, to your spouse simply by naming him or her as the beneficiary.

Source: David Brown, Toronto Star

Or you can give any infirm children or grandchildren under 18 who are dependent upon you the same tax-free gift, without having to pay probate fees. Or you can designate your RRSP to buy an annuity to look after a healthy dependent child or grandchild until he or she reaches age 18.

Other things to mull over:

- If you die without designating your spouse as the beneficiary of your RRSP, but if he or she is the beneficiary of your estate then it's still okay. Your spouse can receive the money by filling out Form T2019 and the RRSP assets will be transferred, tax-free.
- Children stop being children, as CCRA sees it, when they turn 18. Beyond that age you cannot roll your RRSP assets over to them without being taxed (the exception is for an infirm child or grandchild, regardless of age).
- By law, retirement assets are divided equally upon divorce, as they are considered "family assets."

JUST TO RECAP:

- An RRSP is not a product; it is a process.
- An RRSP defers tax; you pay that tax in retirement when you should be in a lower tax bracket.
- Monthly RRSP contributions can lower taxes on your paycheque.
- A yearly RRSP contribution will see you get a tax refund.
- You can contribute to an RRSP until the end of the year in which you turn 69.
- There is no minimum age—as long as you earn income.
- You should file a tax return, even in years when no taxes are due.
- The contribution limit is 18% of the previous year's income to a maximum of $13,500.
- Payments into a company pension plan are deducted from this contribution room.
- Missed contributions can be made at any time.
- You can make a total lifetime overcontribution of $2000; there is no tax refund on an overcontribution.
- You can contribute to your RRSP at any time.
- For any particular tax year, your contribution must be made by the end of February the next year.
- Your refund depends on your particular tax bracket.
- A whole range of investment products are RRSP eligible; certain investments are not.
- You can have more than one RRSP, but it's best to just have one self-directed plan.
- Interest on a loan taken out for RRSP investing is not tax-deductible.
- Most financial institutions will offer RRSP loans at their best rate— prime.
- Your RRSP is allowed to contain up to 25% in foreign securities (30% in the 2001 tax year).
- First-time home buyers can withdraw up to $20,000 ($40,000 with spouse) to buy a house.
- You can contribute to your spouse's RRSP, earning a tax refund while splitting income.
- Transferring plans from one financial institution to another is okay with Canada Customs and Revenue Agency.
- Do not write "estate" as the beneficiary of your RRSP—big tax hit; name your spouse instead.

Chapter 4

Cut tax, build wealth with early, frequent contributions

You can contribute a certain percentage of your earned income every year into an RRSP, to the allowable maximum. Earned income is money earned by working or having rental income, not money your investments have brought in. Only a tiny number of Canadians actually contribute the RRSP maximum each year, because they either do not earn enough or they lack the extra cash.

Action Plan Requirement. . .
One of the very best RRSP strategies is to contribute to your plan early in the tax year. That means you should make your 2001 contribution on Tuesday, January 2, 2001—well before "RRSP Season" in January/February 2002.

How much are you allowed for the 2000 tax year? Your annual T4 slip from your employer arrives in February 2001. And Canada Customs and Revenue Agency (CCRA) will not send you a Notice of Assessment statement of how much you can put into the RRSP, based on 2000 income, until sometime in the summer.

One way is to guess—after all, you can fine-tune your plan later when CCRA eventually does notify you. Or, you can call CCRA's TIPS line:

- The phone number is listed in the government pages of your phone book under Canada Customs and Revenue Agency, Taxation.
- Have last year's tax return handy, along with your social insurance number.
- Talk with the computer for a little while and it will tell you your limit, including missed contributions.

If you are a hands-on type of person who wants the accurate and complicated approach, here we go:

IF YOU DON'T HAVE A COMPANY PENSION PLAN

In 2001 you can contribute 18% of the money earned in 2000, to a maximum of $13,500. Plus, you can catch up on past contributions, as well as overcontribute once to a limit of $2,000.

IF YOU DO HAVE A COMPANY PENSION PLAN

It's the same procedure, but you must take into account your pension adjustment, which can be found in Box 52 of the T4 slip you get in February. You can contribute 18% of your earned income to a maximum of $13,500, less the pension adjustment amount.

HOW TO DETERMINE YOUR "EARNED INCOME"

Here is what qualifies as "earned income":

- Employment earnings
- Self-employment earnings
- Rental income (after expenses, such as mortgage payments)
- Royalties and advances (authors and inventors)
- Research grants
- CPP and QPP disability payments
- Taxable long-term disability payments
- Employee profit-sharing plan allocations
- Supplementary employment-insurance benefits
- Alimony and child support
- Director's fees
- Any taxable benefits showing up on your T4 slip

And here is a partial list of income that does not qualify you to increase your RRSP contribution limit:

- Employment-insurance benefits
- CPP or QPP retirement benefits
- Investment interest (GICs etc.)
- Capital gains
- Dividend income

- Pension income
- Business income as limited partner
- Scholarships or bursaries

Once you have added together all earned income, reduce it by subtracting such things as:

- Union dues
- Alimony payments
- Self-employment losses
- Professional dues
- Deductible employment expenses
- Rental losses

Once you arrive at your earned income, multiply it by 18%, deduct your pension adjustment (if applicable) and that is your allowed 2000 RRSP contribution. It cannot exceed $13,500. Add any unused contribution "room" from the past, and subtract any overcontributions beyond the $2,000 limit.

Here's a ready-made worksheet to help you reach that bottom line:

WORKSHEET FOR CALCULATING EARNED INCOME

Add together:	Line on 2000 tax return	Amount
Total employment earnings (T4 slips)	101-104	_____
Net rental income	104	_____
Alimony or child care income	128	_____
Self-employment income	135-143	_____
Taxable disability payments	114,152	_____
Employee profit-sharing allocation	104	_____
Research grants	104	_____
Supplementary employment-insurance benefits	104	_____
Author or inventor royalties	104	_____
Taxable benefits (from T4)		_____
Total		

Subtract from that:

Union or professional dues	212	_____
Alimony or support payments	220	_____
Rental losses	126	_____
Self-employment losses	135-143	_____
Tax-deductible expenses	229	_____
Total		_____
2000 earned income		_____

WEALTH BUILDER NO. 1: SAVE TAXES

If you earn more than $60,000 a year in Canada, you are considered rich. That's when the top marginal tax rate clicks in and suddenly the government takes 53 cents of every dollar you earn. In the United States, the top marginal tax rate is 39.6%, not 53%—and you don't start paying top bucks until you are earning more than $256,500 a year. Thus, tax planning is four or five times more important to us than it is to Americans.

These days 30% of Canadian families pay more than 62% of all taxes. Our high taxes have resulted in a burgeoning underground economy. But the truth is, you don't have to be a tax cheat or evader to drastically reduce the amount of tax you pay. There are many ways to legally increase your income by decreasing your level of taxation.

Many wealthy Canadians know these strategies, and use them. For example, in 1998 a record amount of money went into RRSPs—well over $30 billion—and recent figures are comparable. But the relative number of people contributing did not increase—it's just the same third of Canadians who have it figured out.

And this is what the RRSP—North America's best tax shelter—is all about. The amount of money you save depends on how much money you put in and your marginal tax rate, which is determined by the combination of federal and provincial income taxes in the area where you live, and varies slightly from province to province. (See complete tax tables in the appendix at the back of this book.)

The current system favours people with higher incomes, because the RRSP contribution reduces taxable income, and therefore the tax payable. The more money you earn, the higher your tax bracket. And the higher the tax bracket you are in, the more you save by making a contribution.

A fact of life. . .

. . .is that almost $50 billion a year in interest on the federal debt must be borne by about 10 million taxpayers, who contribute more into the system than they take out. The Canadian middle class are beasts of financial burden. This is precisely why Canadian taxes are not going down enough, and it is why tax planning is one of the most important things you can possibly do to help ensure your financial future. And nothing reduces taxes like an RRSP contribution.

There is a strong possibility that this may change in the future, with Ottawa adopting a system of tax credits, which would address the idea that some have that wealthier Canadians are receiving a disproportionate RRSP break. But the system as it is today recognizes the fact that upper-income Canadians shoulder a massive amount of the tax burden.

Action Plan Requirement. . .

The most significant thing upper—middle-class taxpayers can do to increase their family incomes—freeing up tens of thousands of dollars to invest in today's booming financial markets—is to maximize annual RRSP contributions.

The sooner money is put into your plan, the faster it will compound. And recognize that basic investing should start inside the RRSP bubble. If you have $10,000 to invest in mutual funds, first put it inside a self-directed RRSP. That will earn you a tax refund of $4,000 to $5,000. Now you have thousands more to put into funds, both inside and outside the retirement savings plan. Next year you can use a portion of your contribution room to move funds into your RRSP from outside it. And just for doing that, you will receive another tax-rebate cheque of about $2,000.

Meanwhile, your funds should give you double-digit annual returns. So, one year after investing $10,000 in a self-directed RRSP, you will have maybe $17,000 in assets.

How much would your salary have to be increased to take home an extra $7,000 this year? In the top tax bracket in Ontario, you'd need a raise of more than $14,000.

Source: David Brown, Toronto Star

Did you know. . .

. . .if you live in a province promising a tax cut next year, and you are in the top tax bracket, an RRSP contribution will be worth more to you in tax savings now than it will next year? So, it makes sense to catch up on missed contributions and make your 2001 contribution now.

DON'T FORGET:

- Earned income is derived by working or from rental property; investment income cannot be included.
- You can contribute 18% of your 2000 earned income, to a maximum of $13,500.
- Contributions to a company pension plan must be subtracted from your contribution room.
- Call CCRA's TIPS line to determine how much room you have in missed contributions.
- Tax planning is an essential component in building your wealth.
- Your RRSP contribution refund is the same percentage as your tax bracket.

Chapter 5

Boring or dazzling:
Get the right RRSP

Most people think an RRSP is a product—an investment on its own—and they believe it always earns interest. RRSPs only earn interest when somebody—through choice or ignorance—puts their money in a no-risk, low-yield savings account or debt security such as a guaranteed investment certificate (GIC). The return is guaranteed and rules are in place to ensure that nobody will lose their first $60,000 in a GIC issued by a bank, broker, trust or credit union that is a member of the Canada Deposit Insurance Corporation.

The GIC-type RRSP is the preferred choice of most Canadians; however, people's thinking regarding RRSP investments is nonetheless starting to change. It has to. Our aging population will simply run out of private retirement funds if it relies on interest-bearing securities to build up its wealth.

In terms of RRSPs, you have three options: boring, better and best. Here's how they compare:

REALLY BORING ONES

At the bottom of the RRSP hierarchy are deposit accounts that pay a ridiculously low rate of interest that moves with the prime, just like your daily interest chequing or savings account rates. These are safe in the sense that the money on deposit will not decrease, and you will be guaranteed up to $60,000 from Ottawa if the financial institution collapses. The overriding danger is that your savings will probably not even rise as much as inflation does, meaning you will suffer a loss in the purchasing power of your retirement nest egg.

ONE STEP UP

Slightly more potent is the GIC RRSP. A fixed rate is one advantage of this product, and it is again insured to the $60,000 limit. You know exactly how much you will earn, and within an RRSP, the interest compounds tax-free. But its advantages are also its drawbacks. Interest earned will be as low as it goes. And in return for the time guarantee, you give up cashability and flexibility. It cannot be cashed in if interest rates rise, so you don't enjoy any of the increase. There is no potential for growth, or capital gain.

Consider this. . .

. . .a far better alternative to a GIC that offers a greater rate of return and even less risk than a GIC, along with the potential for a capital gain and even the ability to cash it in before maturity. They are government strip bonds, and are issued by the federal and provincial governments. Read the section "Why buy a GIC when there are strip bonds?" in Chapter 10.

ZIPPIER GICs

The growing number of disillusioned GICs fans have forced banks to develop new approaches—the new-wave GICs, marketed exclusively in the first couple of months of a new year or in the fall alongside Canada Savings Bonds. Frankly, most are gimmicks. You are still better off 10 times out of 10 investing in quality mainstream mutual funds or a basket of blue-chip stocks. Here's what's out there:

- **For those who think interest rates will be much lower in a year's time**—Extendible GICs. Lock your money up for a year, with the option to extend the one-year rate for another year. Are rates going down? Likely not much. So this is of dubious value.
- **For those who normally buy Canada Savings Bonds**—Redeemable GICs. On sale for a short period when CSBs are marketed, they are just like CSBs—cash them in after a few months and they'll pay a slightly higher rate of return. The advantages are the same as CSBs—a place to park cash for a while and earn more than in a bank savings account. For a long-term investment, forget it.

- **For those who wish interest rates would go up**—Escalating GICs. These give the appearance of high rates. Three years ago, for example, one trust company introduced an escalating rate GIC that went to 10% after seven years. But here's the rub: the blended rate—the average rate of return over all the years the GIC is locked in—is very close to the traditional GIC rate. Sadly, you are taxed on the blended rate—taxes paid in the early years will be more than the return, if not inside an RRSP.

- **For people who want the sizzle of stock markets, but who are wimps**—Market index-related GICs. These increase the rate of return as stocks rise in value. Sounds good, but be careful. Many of these are just marketing creations and, in general, the premium you receive is tiny. The idea is to guarantee investors a minimum rate over a fixed period—usually a rate less than with traditional GICs. Then you get extra if the TSE 300 or the TSE 35 index of the Standard and Poor's 500 index rises.

Action Plan Requirement. . .

Instead of purchasing stock-indexed GICs, you are far better off to invest in the stock market directly through equity-based mutual funds, or stocks themselves, if you have enough capital. These are professionally managed funds that spread investors' risk by investing in scores of various stocks, in Canada, North America or around the world. Not only will you benefit from the long-term growth of the stock market, but you will also be paid income in the form of capital gains, not interest. So if the funds are ever held outside your RRSP, the income they generate will have much less tax exposure.

MUCH BETTER CHOICES

Any mutual fund company can set up a mutual funds RRSP for you, or you can deal with your financial adviser. There are about 2,000 to choose from, many in different categories. When asked how I choose my own assets, my answer is always a surprise to most: I write a cheque to my financial planner and tell him to choose. After all, he's the pro. So far, I have no complaints. For example, my portfolio went up last year, on average, 15%. I'm not greedy. That's enough.

If I were to choose my own funds, at my age (51), the obvious choice would be growth funds—those that are based on the performance of the stock market.

STILL RISK AVERSE?

If you want less risk (although I believe that investing long term in the market is virtually risk-free), then you can put your money into fixed-income mutual funds that invest in bonds as well as mortgages. And if you want some growth as well as fixed-income security, there are balanced funds to consider. They spread their assets among both categories.

All of these funds will give you professional management and more diversification than you could ever get yourself. They have a vastly higher potential for growth than any kind of GIC but of course, unlike a GIC, the returns are not guaranteed. There is more risk.

There is also usually more cost—most funds come with commissions attached, typically a few percentage points of the amount invested. Some funds charge the commission (called a "load") up front when you buy it, while others charge you when fund units are cashed in.

COMMISSION AVERSE?

The thought of paying a commission drives many people into no-load funds such as Altamira, T-D Green Line and other bank funds, or Scudder, to name a few. This is fine for people who want to save a few bucks, and many of the funds that these companies manage have excellent track records. But most no-load funds are also no-help funds. You do not get the expertise of a financial adviser to guide you into the right fund purchase.

Did you know. . .

. . .if you make a one-time investment of $2,000 at age 22, you can amass about $200,000 by the time you hit 70? To do that, though, you must average a return of about 10% a year—GICs and savings bonds won't get you there. If you have the earnings and drive to go for more, $2,000 invested annually earning the same return for the same 48-year period will deliver more than $2 million.

SELF-DIRECTED RRSPs ARE BEST

A self-directed RRSP shelters whatever is inside from tax. It's not run by the bank, like a GIC RRSP, and it's not run by a mutual fund company. Instead, it is run by you. But hopefully, you have the wisdom to have it administered by a financial planner whose advice you trust.

It can cost $100 to $300 a year in administration fees to a financial institution, or a broker. There are also some fees to pay when you transfer your existing RRSP assets into a self-directed plan. Still, this is a cheap way to get the flexibility and control needed to turbo-charge your retirement assets.

HOW DO YOU START?

It's as simple as sitting down with your adviser, broker or banker and filling out some forms. You can do this when making your annual RRSP contribution; or you can open the plan and transfer assets you already own (mutual funds, stocks, GICs, CSBs, and so on), or existing RRSPs from other institutions.

Transfer fees can cost as little as $25 or as much as $100, but don't fret about it. The advantages of having all your retirement assets in one plan will far outweigh the one-time cost.

Keep in mind. . .

. . .institutions are in fierce competition for your money and are loathe to give it up. Notify them as early as possible that a maturing GIC or term deposit will be transferred. Then make sure you have a good paper trail.

To transfer, fill out a T-2033 form (your broker, adviser or banker has it) and have it sent to where the funds are. This will allow the funds to be sent to your self-directed plan without any taxes being deducted. If you don't do this, you run the risk of your RRSP simply being collapsed, and becoming fully taxable.

Make arrangements to go to the bank itself to pick up a cashier's or certified cheque for the amount, and then take it directly to where your self-directed plan is being administered.

WHAT TO PUT IN YOUR
SELF-ADMINISTERED RRSP

The answer depends on your age, assets, risk tolerance, status of your spouse and several other factors. In general, the younger you are, the more heavily invested you should be in stocks and equity mutual funds. As you age, the amount of fixed income should rise.

And, in general, your RRSP assets should be slightly more conservatively managed than assets you hold outside the plan. Why? Because their tax-free status simply means they will perform better, and you need not take as much risk for the same rate of return.

ADD SOME ZING WITH FOREIGN CONTENT

Canada is a great country, but you shouldn't have all your wealth in Canadian dollars. Although the uncertainty surrounding Quebec has abated somewhat, our loonie could tank again when the separatist factions power up the referendum call to arms. Foreign content will provide a valuable buffer during such events.

Then there's the debt. With the federal deficit eliminated, and many provinces also on the road to balanced, or even surplus, budgets, the picture has improved somewhat.

While this is reason to cheer, we still have a massive foreign debt obligation. In fact, we are so deep in it that the Department of Finance has admitted, "We have suffered a tangible loss of economic sovereignty."

Action Plan Requirement. . .

If you have all your wealth in Canadian currency, you will lose purchasing power as interest rates rise—unless you have assets to offset that, assets that rise in value when the dollar falls. In other words, foreign assets—things denominated in other kinds of money.

Every 12 months, we ship almost $30 billion in Canadian currency into the pockets of American, German, Japanese and other bondholders in the form of interest. This is fiscal insanity. Now, you may not be able to change this, but you certainly can shield yourself from the debt disaster that is looming out there beyond the year 2015. And your RRSP is the place to start.

In total, 25% of your RRSP assets can be held as foreign content. That figure jumps to 30% for the 2001 tax year. So on January 1, 2001 your portfolio's foreign content can be boosted to that level. Using clone funds, of course, you can achieve 100% foreign content. More on that later.

A fact of life. . .

. . .is that some Canadian investors believe the foreign content cap is too low, yet their average foreign content holding is only 16%. So says research conducted by the Bank of Nova Scotia. It also discovered that the average Canadian with an RRSP has only 9% foreign content in his or her plan, and 40% of Canadians have no foreign content at all.

You can diversify outside your RRSP, as well as within it, in several ways:

- **Buy into global mutual funds**—They take your Canadian dollars and make investments denominated in foreign currency, while the fund unit price stays in Canadian currency. If the loonie falls, the relative worth of the foreign-currency holdings rises, which buoys the fund unit price, protecting you.
- **Invest in Canadian companies giving you an income stream in other currencies**—For example, when Lucien Bouchard succeeded Jacques Parizeau and became premier of Quebec, I rebalanced my portfolio. One purchase was Royal Bank preferred shares, which paid me dividends in U.S. dollars.
- **If you want the security of fixed-income investments**—You can always buy government bonds denominated in other currencies. These bonds are issued by provincial governments, or by Crown corporations. They pay you interest in German marks or Japanese yen, and there is no need to convert your Canadian dollars into those currencies when you buy.

ANOTHER OPTION—CLONE FUNDS

Perhaps the biggest change in the mutual fund industry over the past couple of years has been the introduction of 100% RRSP-eligible versions of the fund companies' most popular foreign funds. These "clone" funds, as they are called throughout the finance sector, can provide much more exposure to foreign markets than your RRSP previously enjoyed. Their main drawback is cost. Most add another 0.3% to 0.7% to the management expense ratio, which can translate into paying up to an extra 3% on the gains.

MAXING THE 25% ZING

You are currently allowed up to 25% of the "book value" of your RRSP assets to be foreign—book value means the price you originally paid, not the market value today. The book value also includes all fees, loads or commissions you had to pay to acquire those assets.

If your self-administered RRSP is managed by a professional financial adviser or broker (and it should be), then you will receive a regular accounting of the percentage of foreign content. Just make sure it hovers around 24%, giving you a little flexibility.

If you are taking on the task of running your own RRSP, then here's what to remember:

- It's book value that matters, not market value. So if your global mutual funds rise in value, and suddenly amount to $3,000 of your $10,000 RRSP, don't worry. Your book value has not changed.
- CCRA will impose a penalty if your RRSP foreign content rises and stays above 25%. That penalty will be 1% a month on the excess—and it must be paid in precious RRSP-sheltered dollars.

If you go over the limit, then you must:

- Sell enough of the foreign assets to get back on track,
- Deposit more assets into your plan (if you have room available) to reduce the foreign assets to 25%, or
- Swap the excess RRSP assets for non-foreign ones outside your RRSP. In this case, you retain ownership of everything—but be aware of possible tax implications.

WHAT CONSTITUTES FOREIGN CONTENT?

Lots of things qualify:

- Mortgages held on foreign properties, or loaned to foreigners investing in Canada

- Limited partnerships (even if they are Canadian—because they already receive favoured tax treatment)
- Bonds issued by foreign governments (foreign currency-pay bonds issued by Canadian governments are not considered foreign content)
- Stocks of non-Canadian companies, even if they trade on Canadian exchanges.

But for most people, foreign content comes in just one form: mutual funds. One example is global bond funds that invest in a basket of bonds from several countries. This reduces the risk to individual investors and counterbalances against inevitable currency fluctuations.

But there are those who argue eloquently against "wasting" your valuable foreign content space on international bond funds. And it's an argument that makes sense: You can invest in the foreign-pay bonds of Canadian governments, Crown corporations and corporations (as well as a few other institutions, such as the World Bank) to receive the same protection against the falling dollar as the foreign bond funds, but without using any of your 25%. These are all considered Canadian content, even though they pay you in other currencies.

Action Plan Requirement. . .
This is probably the ultimate strategy. Use all your RRSP space for international equity funds—mutual funds that put money into foreign stocks yielding much higher long-term returns and more diversity of assets.

There is no doubting the higher returns of going international. According to the Bank of Montreal, over the last decade, people who invested in Canadian mutual funds earned a total return of about 75%, whereas investors in global funds have enjoyed cumulative returns of up to 500%.

Meanwhile Canadians afraid of losing any of their money earned a glorious 6% on long-term GICs, which was reduced last year by inflation to a real return of about 4.5%. That's not investing.

HOW TO EXCEED THE 25% LIMIT

There are a few legal ways to boost the effective foreign content in your RRSP past 25%. And you should use some or all of these strategies:

- Get as much of an income stream in foreign currency as you want by investing in foreign-pay Canadian bonds—bonds that will pay you interest in American dollars, Swiss francs or other currencies. They are not considered foreign content and are completely RRSP-eligible.
- Choose from several mutual funds that also do this—putting their money into foreign-pay Canadian bonds, making them RRSP-eligible but not being classified as foreign content.
- Use Canadian funds to increase your foreign content, because many of them invest 25% of their cash in foreign assets. So, when you buy them, you are also increasing your foreign exposure. Make sure you research the foreign content level of any Canadian mutual fund you are considering buying.
- Invest in international financial institution bonds issued by outfits such as the World Bank. Denominated in American and other currencies, they are RRSP-eligible without using up foreign content room.
- By holding shares of a Canadian small business in your RRSP, you can boost your allowed foreign content—by double the regular limit. Ottawa will let you increase foreign content by three times the amount you have invested in that small business. The rules used to restrict small business shares to 50% of the value of your RRSP, but now there is no limit.

SPLIT INCOME WITH A SPOUSAL RRSP

A typical scenario for many Canadian families has Dad working for four decades and ending up in the top tax bracket with a good pension or substantial RRSPs. Mom takes time out of the workforce to raise a family, has little retirement income and no personal savings. All of the family's liquid assets are in the hands of Dad, who pays the most tax.

For example, a retired couple in B.C. living on one income of $70,000 will see $22,000 evaporate in taxes. But if that one income could be split into two incomes of $35,000, the family tax savings would be almost $9,000, because they are both in a lower tax bracket. To earn $9,000 after 40% tax, you'd have to have a five-year GIC yielding 6%, worth $250,000.

HOW TO SPLIT INCOME

Canada Customs and Revenue Agency does not allow you to just give money to your spouse. It has rules—called attribution rules—that attribute earned or investment income back to you in most cases. One of the best ways around this is to contribute to a spousal RRSP. This simply means putting money into a plan that your mate owns, and when he or she cashes the plan out, the money is taxed at your spouse's (usually) lower rate.

What's a spouse? According to the government, a spouse is "a person of the opposite sex to whom the individual is married or with whom the individual has cohabited in a conjugal relationship for a period of at least one year, or less than one year if the two individuals are the natural or adoptive parents of a child."

Consider this. . .

. . .just about all of today's middle-class baby boomers, Generation Xers and echo boomers will see no government cheques in retirement. Only the disabled and destitute will be cared for. The rest of us must be smart as we prepare. And being smart means going spousal.

If you are gay or lesbian, this definition might include you in the near future now that Parliament has amended the Human Rights Act to outlaw discrimination against sexual orientation. For the rest of us, here's how it works today:

- Once you find out how much you can contribute to your RRSP this year, you have a choice: Put it all in your own plan, put it all in a plan in your spouse's name, or split it between the two.
- You can reduce your taxable income by the amount of the spousal RRSP contribution.
- Your spousal contribution in no way affects your spouse's ability to contribute to his or her own plan, based on income. Just don't both of you contribute money to the same plan—the accounting is too complex when it comes to attribution for tax purposes.
- You can open a spousal plan any place where a normal RRSP is offered—it does not cost extra.
- When you open the plan, make it clear that it's for your spouse.

- Money must remain in the spousal plan for three years before it is considered his or hers. After that time, your spouse can withdraw the money at any time, and it will be taxed at his or her rate.
- If you withdraw money before the three years are up, it will be attributed back to you and taxed in your hands.
- If you are the higher-income earner on the downsizing block, then the attribution rule can work in your favour. If you are laid off, your spouse can withdraw money from his or her plan before three years are up and it will be attributed to you and taxed at your rate—which, when unemployed, will be low.
- There is one circumstance under which spousal money can be withdrawn early with no attribution back to the contributor, and that's under the Home Buyers' Plan when you use it for a down payment.
- You can continue putting money into a spousal RRSP and get a break on your own taxes, regardless of your age, as long as your mate is 69 or younger.
- When your spouse reaches age 69, the spousal RRSP can be converted into a RRIF.
- Besides helping you to effectively split income in retirement and saving taxes, a spousal RRSP can also help avoid the clawback on the existing Old Age Security and the Age Tax Credit. By using a spousal RRSP, you can even out your two incomes and reduce the clawback.

A fact of life. . .

Anyone reading this book who is my age (51), or younger, can pretty much forget about OAS, GIS, the Age Credit and any other pension benefit that Ottawa comes up with. These programs are luxuries that Canada will no longer be able to afford two decades from now.

DIVORCE, SEPARATION OR MARITAL BREAKDOWN

Canadian law deals quickly and decisively with retirement assets when the marriage or common-law relationship fails. In this instance, a spousal RRSP is treated the same as your own plan. While the money you put in your spouse's plan over the years legally belongs to him or her, when separation or divorce occurs, all retirement assets are deemed property of both spouses, regardless of who put in what.

SUMMARY:

What you should do:
- Closely examine stock index-linked GICs before buying.
- Invest directly into the market via equity-based mutual funds; beats new GICs by far.
- Use one self-directed RRSP to protect your assets.
- Move any existing RRSPs and assets into your self-directed plan.
- Have your plan administered by a trusted financial adviser.
- When transferring a plan, stay on top of things; have a readily available paper trail.
- Have RRSP assets slightly more conservatively managed than those outside of your plan.
- Ensure that your RRSP has the maximum amount of foreign content allowed.
- Invest in Canadian companies that provide an income stream in other currencies.
- Buy government bonds denominated in other currencies if you want security of fixed income.
- Explore adding 100% RRSP-eligible versions or clones of popular foreign funds.
- Look for Canadian mutual funds that max out their foreign investment.
- Invest in international financial institution bonds that are RRSP-eligible.
- Use a spousal RRSP to split income.

What *not* to do:
- Avoid interest-bearing securities, especially low-interest GICs and savings bonds.
- Avoid savings RRSPs; they just won't do the trick.
- Don't use GICs or Canada Savings Bonds for long-term investments.
- Don't have all your wealth in Canadian dollars.
- Don't be like 40% of Canadians with RRSPs who have no foreign content in their plans.
- Don't expect any government cheques in retirement if you are younger than 50.

Chapter 6

No cash? No problem.
Potent RRSP strategies

The RRSP is a simple instrument, and yet there are many strategies, options, possibilities and a tremendous number of mind-numbing details to grasp, absorb and put into action. That is why I always urge anyone with the least bit of interest in their financial future to make use of a qualified financial adviser. They know this stuff.

However, familiarity with the many facets of RRSPs will help you productively discuss your needs with your financial planner, and ensure that the strategy developed works for you.

Here are a few suggestions to make your RRSP the extremely potent financial tool that it is.

YOU DON'T NEED CASH TO CONTRIBUTE

Canada Customs and Revenue Agency (CCRA) will pay you money to shelter assets you already own from tax. Any financial security that qualifies to be in an RRSP can be put into a plan at any time, instead of cash. Assets that you already own can be used as a contribution (up to your yearly limit), or you can transfer assets into your plan to use up the carry-forward on unused past contributions.

Action Plan Requirement. . .

Don't sit on taxable investments that could be both free of tax and leveraged much higher in value. It's time to examine your portfolio. Write down all the assets you own and whether any of them qualify to go into a self-directed RRSP. If you have not made this year's contribution, or if you have unused contribution room from previous years, then call your financial adviser and make a contribution in kind.

For doing that, the government will send you money—because the contribution of assets you already own will be treated the same way as a cash contribution. CCRA calls this a "contribution in kind."

CONTRIBUTIONS IN KIND

Here's what qualifies:

- Canada Savings Bonds
- Corporate bonds
- Government bonds
- GICs
- Mutual fund units
- Limited partnership units
- Provincial savings bonds
- Mortgages
- Small business shares
- Stocks
- Term deposits
- Strip bonds
- Treasury bills
- Cash
- Cashable GICs

As you can see, many types of securities can go into your RRSP in lieu of cash. Consider how much better off a middle-aged couple would be in retirement if every year they took a chunk of their portfolio and tax-sheltered it via a contribution in kind, especially into a spousal RRSP if one partner is in a lower tax bracket.

Consider this. . .

That stocks and stock funds, over the long term, have historically outperformed other investment classes. Between 1956 and 1996—from a boom time, followed by many years of economic turmoil, to the beginning of another boom time—the value of stocks, according to the TSE 300's average annual compound return, rose by 9.96% each year. That's almost 1.4% more than the annual average growth of bonds as measured by the ScotiaMcLeod Long Term Government Bond Index.

SOME RULES TO REMEMBER:

- Start with a self-directed RRSP—no need to administer it yourself, that's the job of your financial adviser. Never get talked into a low-paying GIC RRSP when you make an RRSP contribution.
- You can't make a contribution in kind larger than your annual RRSP limit, plus any carry-forward room from previous years.
- The asset you contribute in kind must be properly valued. If it's mutual fund units, then the market value on the day of transfer is the value, not the price you first paid for them. If it's a strip bond, the same applies. Canada Savings Bonds are credited for both the face value and compound interest.
- CCRA stipulates that when an asset is transferred into your RRSP, it's as if it was sold. If it has risen in value, you may have a tax liability. In the case of a stock or mutual fund, for example, that could generate a capital gain, which must be included in your taxable income for the year.
- However, if an asset has declined in value since you bought it, don't transfer it directly into your RRSP because you will not be able to claim a capital loss. Instead, sell the security and then use the cash to make the RRSP contribution. Now you can claim that capital loss against any capital gains.
- The rules also allow you to substitute assets that are currently inside your self-directed RRSP for assets that you own on the outside—as long as they are qualifying assets. For example, if you needed cash you could borrow it from your RRSP. That means you could transfer mutual fund units held outside the plan for assets inside that could be converted to cash (Canada Savings Bonds, for example). So, you get the cash you need without having had to sell the funds—as you avoid triggering a capital gain.
- You can use the substitution rule to fine-tune your RRSP, in order to ensure you have the right stuff inside. For example, if you have investments that pay interest (GICs, for example) or that do not give you annual income but on which you still need to pay annual tax (like strip bonds), then these should be the first things stowed in the RRSP. Investments, such as stocks that pay you dividends, should be on the outside because inside the RRSP you can't use the dividend tax credit, which saves tax. Substituting one asset for another doesn't affect your annual contribution limit but it doesn't earn a tax rebate. There is no restriction on how often you want to swap assets, but some institutions will charge a fee.

YOU CAN MOVE MONEY INSIDE PLANS

It's possible to move money between different RRSPs that you own, from an RRSP to a RRIF (registered retirement income fund) or vice versa, or from a pension plan to or from an RRSP. The rules are reasonable, but also complicated, and you should certainly get professional advice before doing so. Here are some more considerations:

- Money can move tax-free between an RRSP and a RRIF under certain circumstances. If you withdraw too much money from a RRIF, for example, you can transfer the excess back into an RRSP, if you are under age 70 and have contribution room. Or, RRSP money can be used to set up a RRIF at any time. Of course, the only place that RRIF money can come from is an RRSP, an annuity or another RRIF.
- A lump sum of money can be transferred from a registered pension plan into an RRSP, but it must be done directly. You can't get the pension money and then put it in your RRSP without being dinged for tax.
- The same is true for transfers of retirement or severance packages (see Chapter 12). The money must go directly into your RRSP. If you take a cheque, you'll lose up to 30% in taxes right off the top.
- There are only a couple of instances when money can be transferred from your own RRSP into somebody else's—when your marriage goes bust or when you expire.

In the instance of marital breakdown, the law requires that retirement assets be split evenly. That means RRSP money can be transferred directly into your ex-spouse's plan (or RRIF). For this to happen, you must be living apart, and your significant other must meet the definition of "spouse"—the opposite sex, married or common-law, or with whom you've had a child. If you get back together again, the retirement assets may revert to your spouse's plan—which is an interesting form of income splitting.

As for death, CCRA deems this the cashing out of your RRSP or RRIF, and your estate must pay tax on the whole amount, which is a good argument for spending it all before you figuratively cash out.

If your spouse has an RRSP, the money goes there tax-free after your passing. If he or she does not have an RRSP, then the money is taxable.

And if there is no spouse, a child or grandchild may be designated, but only if nobody else has claimed a tax credit for that child, and the child's income was under $6,456, or if he or she was physically or mentally disabled. In these cases, the assets can flow into an RRSP tax-free. Also a dependent child under 18 can receive funds tax-free to purchase an annuity until reaching age 18.

Action Plan Requirement. . .

If you want to leave money for others, the easiest way is to designate your spouse as beneficiary. After death, the assets will simply and quickly flow to him or her. It's worth checking now that you have done this in the proper place on your RRSP documents.

Otherwise, the money can be used to purchase an annuity for the child, through a formula based on his or her age. This is an integral part of estate planning, and the best advice I can give is this: long before you give up the ghost, make sure you plan the disposition of your estate, and do this with a professional.

YOU CAN CARRY UNUSED CONTRIBUTIONS FORWARD

Because CCRA did away with the limits on how much contribution room you can carry forward, you may be tempted to use your money now to pay down the mortgage, or buy a top-of-the-line Porsche, secure in the knowledge that you can catch up on retirement savings later. But, you'd be living a lie.

First, you lose all that tax-free compounding time on money you should have put in—time that can never be caught up in terms of growth. Second, if you keep delaying your contributions, and suddenly the unlimited carry-forward provision is restricted again, that's gonna hurt. Then it may be almost impossible to ensure that you have sufficient money for retirement.

Already Canadians are vastly behind in savings contributions. Why are we leaving 80% or more of the allowable contributions (and huge tax savings) sitting on the table each year? There are several reasons:

- Following the 1990s recession, family finances were too tight for a retirement contribution.
- Canadians are generally unaware that, given cheap interest rates and rising financial markets, it makes perfect sense to borrow for the annual RRSP contribution.

- Not enough people are doing it the easy way—making monthly contributions through pre-approved bank plans or payroll deductions.
- Ignorance of the fact that you can make a contribution in kind.
- Carry-forward rules give a false sense of security, making it less urgent to contribute regularly.

Whatever the reason, this has created a serious situation, when we are meeting only 20% or less of the goal. And that's exactly what the annual contribution limit is—the goal.

Did you know. . .

. . .RRSP limits do not come out of a hat? They have been carefully created by actuaries to meet assumptions about demographics, income needs, future economic conditions and public pensions.

The RRSP contribution limit is the recommended amount that you should be putting away every year, without significantly altering your lifestyle. The assumption is that you will contribute for 35 years. So, if you're over 30 and don't have an RRSP, you're already behind. Many people are staggeringly behind—well into their forties and early fifties with little or nothing saved.

Middle-aged baby boomers have socked away little more than $30,000 on average—in Canada, not enough to finance one year in retirement. Many will never be able to make up that lost ground. And as for waiting for inheritances to do the trick, that financial legacy is currently being spent by the longest-living and healthiest senior generation in North American history. In fact, many boomers will be reaching retirement with their parents still alive.

Here are some more strategies regarding the carry-forward provision:

- Younger taxpayers raising a family or paying down real estate could save up unused RRSP contributions until they are in a higher tax bracket, and therefore earning a bigger refund. The danger here is that you don't get into the habit of making RRSP contributions. You are not building up savings that can compound, tax-free, for that extra period of time.
- There's also the danger of building up carry-forward that you will never be able to use. It doesn't take many years of missed contributions to amass a great deal of unused contribution room.

- If you come into an inheritance, be careful about how you use your carry-forward allowance. Dumping a great deal of money into an RRSP could temporarily drop you into a lower tax bracket, meaning a smaller refund. Or, it could make you subject to the alternative minimum tax, which was introduced in 1986 to ensure that wealthy people could not use deductions to reduce their taxable income to zero.
- Failing to make a regular annual contribution means losing annual tax refunds. Remember, if you are in the 40% tax bracket, a $10,000 contribution earns you a $4,000 cheque from Ottawa—money that can then be reinvested in your retirement plan (using the carry-forward), or used to pay down an RRSP loan.
- But the most damaging aspect of postponing your RRSP contribution is the lost earnings that result from the tax-free compounding of assets.

Action Plan Requirement. . .

Today's baby boomers should make use of their carry-forward immediately, and then get on a regular schedule of RRSP contributions, ideally monthly and by automatic withdrawal.

THE COST OF NOT CONTRIBUTING

The carry-forward provision is a gift for those who are behind. Make sure you do catch up. Borrow to do this, or use contributions in kind, putting the tax refund into your plan because:

- The ability to carry forward unused contributions could end at any time.
- The addition of each unused contribution makes it that much harder to ever get all that money into your plan.
- You are losing out on the greatest power of the RRSP—assets compounding value, tax-free, over a long period.
- You are foregoing annual tax-rebate cheques that can increase your wealth.
- You're gambling that you will be in a higher tax bracket later, when just the opposite could be the case.
- You will keep falling behind, and may reach a point where you can never catch up.

MAKING AN OVERCONTRIBUTION

The law cuts you some slack by allowing your RRSP to have more money in it than the rules normally allow. It used to be a sizeable whack of money—up to $8,000 in a cumulative lifetime overcontribution.

Then in the 1995 budget Ottawa chopped it down to $2,000. The penalty for having more than the allowed amount of money in your RRSP is a charge of 1% a month on the excess contribution, until you get rid of it. The penalty must be paid within three months of the end of the year in which you had the excess. Miss that deadline and CCRA will also hit you with arrears.

As a matter of fact. . .

. . .if you're my age (51) and you overcontribute $2,000 and manage to average 10% a year (not difficult with conservative, equity-based mutual funds), by age 69, it will have grown into $13,000. If you are fortunate enough to be 29 years old, and overcontribute the same amount at the same rate of return, when you're 69 it will have turned into more than $90,000!

You can have that $2,000 overcontribution living inside your plan for decades—and then use it as part of an annual contribution, getting a tax refund. So, who is ideally suited to use an overcontribution strategy? Just about anyone:

- Young people. The younger the better, starting at 19, which is the minimum age for carrying an overcontribution. It makes sense for parents to make an overcontribution in the name of a child who does not have earned income and can't contribute to his or her own plan. No tax deduction, but by the time that child reaches the age of 59, he or she will be wealthier by about $90,000, thanks to your gift.
- Retired people, who still have earned income (such as rental income) can overcontribute, and then get the tax deduction back, even if your RRSP has been converted into a RRIF. As long as you continue to have that income, claim the deduction yearly at the rate of 18% of what you are earning—until the full $2,000 is used up. The same thing goes for spousal RRSPs, as long as your spouse is 69 or younger. You can make an overcontribution, then get the money back in deductions from your earned income.

Source: Toronto Sun

- However, if you make the overcontribution before you retire, and don't have earned income, the money will be taxed twice. First, because you didn't get a refund when it went into the plan (it was already in after-tax dollars), and second, when it comes out of your RRIF as income.
- Another reason for everyone to carry an overcontribution is to give a little personal protection in case you are unexpectedly laid off or incapacitated. Next year you might qualify to make an RRSP contribution (based on this year's earnings) but if you're out of work, it's unlikely you'd have the money. In that case, claim the $2,000 overcontribution that you've been carrying as your RRSP contribution. That will earn you a refund cheque, just when you could use it.

Action Plan Requirement. . .

An overcontribution makes perfect sense as long as you're careful to avoid exceeding the $2,000 limit. The real purpose is to get as much money as possible into your plan for the longest period of time, at the highest rate of return. If you do make an overcontribution, don't be content to have it earning 4% or 5% in a fixed-income investment. Go for a growth mutual fund with the potential of doubling your money twice every decade.

THE RISK TO REALLY FEAR

Every year Canadians contribute just a fraction of what they could to their RRSPs, for reasons already discussed. But, compounding the mistake, is that those who do contribute end up wimping out because they are afraid of taking a risk. They end up investing tax-sheltered retirement funds in GICs or savings bonds. Both, in my view, are a disaster and likely to remain so for the next decade.

Here's what I believe:

- The North American economy is and will continue growing strongly, thanks to demographics.
- Inflation will be no real threat.
- Central banks want lower interest rates.
- GICs withdrawn today at low rates will probably come up for renewal at even lower rates.
- Aging baby boomers are about to gorge themselves on mutual funds and equities to get the double-digit returns they so badly need.
- This will accelerate the shift from real assets (your home) to financial assets (stocks/mutual funds).
- Stock markets will continue to climb, albeit with corrections—sometimes massive—along the way. But, over time, there is no real risk in the market with quality investments.
- We are all living extraordinarily long lives. If you are in your thirties or forties today, you could have more than 30 years in retirement to finance.
- Government pensions are an endangered species. Don't count on one.

The greatest threat we all face is outliving the pool of money we are amassing for decades in retirement. The economic fundamentals that are now in high gear demonstrate that the real risk is not losing money—it's not growing it fast enough. Too few Canadians realize that yet, so they continue to invest their RRSP money in the wrong places, and also opt for the wrong asset mix.

ALLOCATING YOUR ASSETS

Where should your RRSP invest? You have three basic choices, or classes of assets. Each has a different level of risk and return associated to it:

1. **Cash equivalents**—Low risk and low return. These are liquid investments that can be converted to cash quickly and on which it is impossible to actually lose money. Included are Canada Savings Bonds, provincial savings bonds, short-term bank deposits, T-bill and money market mutual funds.

2. **Fixed-income**—Low to medium risk, low to moderate return. These pay you regular income at a fixed rate, but vary significantly in their flexibility. The three main contenders are GICs, bond or mortgage funds and government bonds (not savings bonds):

   • Most people choose GICs because they spell out how much money you will have upon maturity and they are insured against loss up to $60,000. Some serious drawbacks, though: interest rates are low, the money is locked up for years, and there's no potential for a capital gain.

   • Bond and mortgage funds are mutual funds that invest in pools of government bonds or residential mortgages; they are attractive to people who want low risk and predictable yield. Many investors do not realize that these funds are a sorry place to have money when interest rates rise because they drop in value.

   • Government bonds are a much better choice. You can buy regular government bonds that pay you interest on a periodic basis, or strip bonds—bonds that have had the interest stripped from them, so they pay no income but are bought at a big discount to face value. The advantages over a GIC are extreme—better rate of interest, cashable anytime, yield a capital gain if interest rates fall, and 100% government guaranteed.

3. **Growth assets**—Higher risk, much higher return. These assets earn capital gains and appreciate much faster—but are also vulnerable to short-term declines. They are best for the buy-and-hold investor who realizes building RRSP assets is a long-term project. The two you should concentrate on are:

   • Equities, also known as stocks. You take on an equity, or ownership, position in a company when you buy its stock, or shares. These are traded in a variety of ways and constantly change in value according to the economy, the company's performance and supply and demand. While the stock market has marched steadily higher over the last 100 years, not all stocks have gained and there have been severe corrections lasting years. Risk varies greatly—invest in bank stocks and receive steady, moderate growth, or choose a dot-com stock and get rich quick, or perhaps destitute, in a few months.

- Mutual funds are pools of assets managed by professionals. Instead of trying to choose your own stocks you buy units in a fund that invests in dozens, or hundreds, of stocks. Funds can invest in all kinds of things, and there are about 2,000 to choose from. It might seem like an impossible task to choose four or six so that's why it's best left to your adviser. The important thing? Concentrate on long-term growth.

HOW MUCH TO ALLOCATE

If you are in your twenties or thirties, there is nothing wrong with putting 100% of your retirement savings into high-octane, equity-based mutual funds.

In your forties and fifties, being 60% into equity funds with the rest in fixed income is still a conservative strategy.

And as for senior investors, they also need growth. The prevailing wisdom that seniors should invest only in fixed-income, such as GICs, is simply wrong. Anybody under the age of 80 should have growth assets.

LIFE AFTER RRSPs: CONVERT TO A RRIF

Okay, now you have been a good, if somewhat untraditional, Canadian, used all the neat RRSP strategies, saved and invested like a crazed beaver and have built up a sizeable retirement nest egg. You are approaching age 69. What next? The rules state that this is the end of your RRSP. You are no longer allowed to make contributions—now you have to start withdrawing money. That can be done in one of three ways:

Cash out and be taxed to the max
Option one is to simply cash in all or part of your RRSPs by collapsing the plans. The result? A huge income tax hit—up to 30% will be withheld at source. Not the wisest move, but there are still some Canadians who might feel it's best to take the money, pay the tax, and run.

Or, go for cash for life
The second option is to use the money in your RRSP to buy an annuity from an insurance company, bank or trust. By giving over a lump sum of money, you receive monthly cheques in return for as long as you live (a life annuity) or for a defined period (fixed-term annuity).

Did you know. . .

. . .that about 56% of Canadians between age 65 and 70 have RRSPs? When the rule change dropped the age of conversion to age 69, more than 400,000 individuals had to convert their RRSPs—up substantially from the previous year's 130,000. The Royal Bank reports that the average portfolio of its clients with maturing RRSPs is worth $35,000 to $45,000.

The amount of money you receive will depend on your age, health, prevailing interest rates and life expectancy. The younger and healthier you are, the less you receive. With a life annuity, the payments continue until you die, unless you have a joint and last survivor annuity, in which case payments continue until the last spouse expires. No payments are made into the estate or to beneficiaries.

With a fixed-term annuity, you usually receive cheques until age 90, or you can base it on your spouse's age, if he or she is younger. Also available are "boutique" annuities, such as ones indexed to inflation or a higher impaired annuity if you are in rough shape and likely to die sooner than the charts predict. And you can use non-RRSP money to purchase a prescribed annuity—which is a way of converting money in mutual funds or bonds, while leaving your RRSP assets to do what they really should, and that is. . .

Best convert to a flexible RRIF

Consider a RRIF as a reverse RRSP. That is, you must start withdrawing money as contributions are no longer accepted. And after the first year, the amount you withdraw is determined by formula.

Of course, you pay tax on what's called the minimum annual payout (MAP). Taxes are not withheld by the bank or trust, like an RRSP, but the MAP is considered income and your marginal rate applies. So, for anyone with income of over $60,000, you will lose half the amount withdrawn.

That's the bad news. The good news is that a RRIF is as flexible and generous as an RRSP in its ability to allow the assets in there to grow and compound free of tax. So, you should have your RRIF set up as a self-directed fund and be following the same growth strategies as your RRSP did.

Since RRIFs were created in 1978, the rules have changed several times to make them more effective:

- You can have as many RRIFs as you want. But—like your RRSP— one big self-directed one is best.
- The money no longer must be withdrawn by age 90. Now a RRIF can be structured to give you income during your entire life.
- You can set up a RRIF at any age.

But the trade-off for this flexibility has been a higher required MAP in the early years of retirement. Here are the rules dictating how much money you have to withdraw.

Under the age of 69

Remember: you can set up a RRIF regardless of your age, and the amount you must withdraw is less, the younger you are. You are also allowed to have the minimum payments based on your spouse's age— which is great if you married young. Just make sure you choose that option when the RRIF is first set up.

Here's the formula:

$$\frac{\text{Value of your RRIF}}{\text{90 minus your age at beginning of year}} = \text{Minimum payment}$$
$$\text{(or your spouse's)}$$

For example, if you are 65 and have $200,000 in your RRIF, then your minimum annual payment will be $200,000 divided by 90 minus 65 (which is 25), which equals $8,000. If your spouse is 55, then the MAP is equal to $200,000 divided by 90 minus 55 (35), which equals $5,714. Clearly, you are miles ahead in terms of deferring tax by having your spouse's age used instead of your own.

Over the age of 69

While the government dropped the age at which you have to convert your RRSP into a RRIF by two years to age 69, the formula for calculating minimum income stays the same until age 71—as above.

After the age of 71, a specified percentage of your RRIF must be taken as income. There is no getting around this, but by using your younger spouse's age, the MAP can be reduced and more of your RRIF capital preserved to keep on growing tax-free inside the fund. Each year a new calculation is made by your bank, trust company or adviser to adjust the amount of income you must take in that year.

Here are the minimum payments, by age.

Age	Annual payment must be equal to this % of RRIF
71	7.38%
72	7.48
73	7.59
74	7.71
75	7.85
76	7.99
77	8.15
78	8.33
79	8.53
80	8.75
81	8.99
82	9.27
83	9.58
84	9.93
85	10.33
86	10.79
87	11.33
88	11.96
89	12.71
90	13.62
91	14.73
92	16.12
93	17.92
94 and over	20.00

You can see the tax bite grows steadily as you age, to the point when 20% of your assets must be taken as income each year in your nineties. At that rate, the RRIF dwindles fast. But should you still be alive and kicking at that age, chances are your cash requirements will be very high—especially in the future when more health care is privatized and the state can no longer afford subsidized institutional care.

That means a RRIF is important, but it should not be your only source of retirement income. So past the age of 80 or so it would make sense to take a chunk of RRIF money and convert it to a life annuity. That would bring down the minimum RRIF payments and give you an assured monthly cheque for life. But, there are other considerations if you are concerned about your estate.

When you cease to be a taxpayer

If there's any good news about dying, this may be it: Money in a RRIF gives you better estate protection than an annuity, which usually comes to an abrupt end when you do. Always make it clear when you set up the RRIF who the beneficiary will be, and back that up with a further declaration in your will.

If you designate your spouse, then regular annual payouts can simply start flowing to him or her, or the spouse can collapse the plan, take all the money (and pay all the taxes) and go on a world cruise. Alternatively, a younger spouse (under the age of 69) can roll the RRIF assets into his or her RRSP, or the RRIF can be collapsed and then restructured into a new RRIF according to the spouse's wishes.

And if you do not name a beneficiary at all, the RRIF is cashed on your demise, with the money rolled into your estate and treated as income in that year. It's a good thing you won't be around to see that tax bill!

REMEMBER:

- Use assets that you already own to use up your contribution space and unused RRSP room.
- There is no limit on the RRSP carry-forward room—use it before you lose it.
- Do you have lots of carry-forward room? Borrow to fill it up, get a big refund, and let your investments compound.
- Make that overcontribution. Don't forget, it's only $2,000 not $8,000 anymore.
- If you are in your thirties or forties, you could have to finance more than 30 years in retirement.
- Government bonds will always be a better choice than low-wattage GICs.
- Concentrate on long-term growth; tune out all the short-term noise.
- The further away from retirement, the more growth assets you should have.
- When you turn 69, you must convert your RRSP into a RRIF.
- Whether it's an RRSP or a RRIF, make clear who the beneficiary will be.

Chapter 7

Your house:
A non-performing asset?

When interest rates began to decline about five years ago, many more people were able to achieve the great Canadian dream—buy a home, pay it off and upon retirement, have a tidy little nest egg on hand.

Sorry. Despite healthy real estate activity over the past few years, the 1980s boom, just like rampant inflation, is not returning. Values of many properties across Canada still may never match their asking price 12 years back, despite an improving housing market. Much of the recent boom can be attributed to pent-up demand cut loose by the lowest interest rates in a generation and lots of first-time buyers.

As a matter of fact. . .

. . .real estate giant Royal LePage says that its research shows that only about 6% of individuals who come into an inheritance will use it to buy a home. In the next 20 years, it is estimated that approximately $50 billion will be transferred annually via inheritances.

The long-term outlook for real estate is slower appreciation than in the past 40 years. Some niche markets will continue to do well—luxury condos, desirable neighbourhoods, prime cottage properties, and so on. However, the average Canadian home will not grow in value quite as quickly as most investment vehicles.

Nevertheless, your home can still be a valuable asset:

- It can give a massive boost to the financial means you will need down the line.
- You have to live somewhere.
- Today's mortgage rates are making it cheaper to buy a home than to rent in any major city, with the exception of Vancouver.

Here are some of my thoughts on RRSP options available to home-owners.

YOUR MORTGAGE VS. YOUR RRSP: NO CONTEST

Is it better to build up an RRSP or pay down a mortgage? Most financial advisers straddle the fence, saying mortgage debt is expensive, non-deductible and the longer you have a home loan the more interest you pay. They also say the more years your money compounds tax-free within an RRSP, the greater the chances you will retire comfortably. The blended approach advises making your maximum RRSP contribution annually and paying down mortgage principal with the refund. It works, but it's slow. I have a better strategy rooted in the firm belief that residential real estate has no long-term future as an investment.

Action Plan Requirement. . .
You should only invest in residential real estate during the first half of your life, more as a forced-savings plan than a way to build capital. In the second half of your life, sell or use the equity through leverage.

WHY DIVERSIFY?

Residential real estate faces a steady, relentless erosion of value. Although some regions of the country have experienced a mini-boom of late it is a deceptive market, based on first-time buyers giving some scared boomers the chance to bail. Price erosion will continue; at the very best, prices will stay the same.

This is because all over the industrialized world, especially in Canada with its rapidly aging population, the trend is away from real assets and towards financial assets, and real estate is a real asset. This trend will explode higher in this new millennium and will only serve to drive real asset values lower.

> ## A fact of life. . .
>
> . . .is that most Canadians have most of their wealth in the wrong type of assets—namely, their homes. Demand will decline. Real estate isn't dead, but it's changing. Demographics will drastically shrink the number of potential buyers. Baby boomers now reaching age 50 will start to obsess with earning double-digit RRSP returns, and realize they are sitting on tens or hundreds of thousands of dollars in their homes, earning them nothing. Then it will be a race to see who can get out of residential real estate the fastest, before the value of some real estate—large, suburban homes, for example—simply evaporates.

The universe of buyers to maintain real estate values is thinning. Here's why:

- Bummed out by uncertain employment prospects and the likelihood of an economic depression in the middle of their working lives, Generation Xers are in no mood to take on massive mortgage debt.
- Immigration has been a bright spot in markets such as Vancouver, but many immigrant families tend to be larger and multi-generational, with the move to individual real estate much slower.
- And the baby boomers—all nine million of them—generally are living in the largest homes of their lives, unlikely to move up and just about certain to move down.

WHY BUY?

So, why invest in real estate right now? Well, you have to live somewhere. For a young person buying a starter home, it's a way to build up equity in the kind of house that will have a better resale future—a townhouse, condo or bungalow near services, which will appeal to aging boomers 10 years from now.

Buying is also a way to stabilize housing costs. But for middle-aged people and older, real estate is a potential financial sinkhole. That equity should be transferred into financial assets. You needn't sell your home—just don't have so much of your net worth in one vulnerable asset. In other words, diversify.

> ### Action Plan Requirement. . .
> Maximize your RRSP contribution, regardless of your age. Then if you are a younger homeowner, apply the tax refund to the mortgage and pay it off in the shortest possible time—but don't stop there. Use the other techniques such as weekly payments, which can shave more than a decade from the time it takes to retire a mortgage.

Younger investors can afford a lot more risk than older ones. So, first-time homebuyers who put money into RRSPs should be investing in growth assets—stocks, equity-based mutual funds, international growth funds, emerging market, Asian and Latin funds. Time is on the side of the young investor, and time always defeats risk.

Will $100,000 equity in your house grow into $2 million two decades from now? Actually, I think you'll be lucky to get your money out, with more than a small premium for inflation.

AFTER YOU ARE 40

Since the Second World War, rising real estate values meant a lot of people didn't have to save and plan for retirement. Besides, "retirement" 20 years ago meant 8 or 10 years. Now it can be 30. So those approaching middle age should have at least half their net worth outside their house, increasing that as they near retirement.

> ### Did you know. . .
> . . .that almost 60% of Canadians who have paid off the mortgage don't have an RRSP! It's almost unforgivable.

Remember, real estate is illiquid—you can't cash it in unless you persuade somebody to buy it. Most people forget this and end up selling at the wrong time, forced to sell by circumstances—and usually at a fire-sale price. Real estate is not an appropriate asset for most seniors. It can end up destroying wealth—trapping it in bricks and mortar and eating it up in maintenance, insurance, taxes and utilities.

With every passing year, your assets have a shorter time to grow. You will be further ahead accumulating them than adding to your home equity. If real estate values decline, the loss doesn't come off the mortgage—it comes off the equity.

If you are in your thirties or more likely your forties, and have built up equity in your home, it's time to start using it. There are several ways of doing this, but one of the easiest is to contact your bank and get a home equity loan—a form of mortgage that will give you cash to invest. Here's why:

- Residential real estate has no secure long-term future.
- Don't get stuck with an expensive asset that you can't sell unless you throw away a pile of equity.
- The interest you pay on a home equity loan is tax-deductible.

USING YOUR EQUITY

Here's an example of the true cost of a home equity loan used for investment purposes:

Equity loan rate:	6%
Your tax rate:	54%
Rate write-off:	3.24%
Actual, after-tax loan rate:	2.76%

Where else could you find $50,000 or $100,000 with one phone call at the effective after-tax rate of just over 2.76%? By using your home equity and then investing the money in quality mutual funds, you will suddenly see the money that used to be earning zero in your house suddenly making double-digit returns.

Is this a dangerous strategy? Some say yes. And when I suggested this strategy in *2015: After the Boom*, critics and skeptics had a hard time surrendering their inflationary notions that real estate is a growing storehouse of wealth, and the stock market is not the place where careful Canadians invest.

But it's that kind of attitude that will keep many Canadians dependent in their old age on the dwindling support of stretched-to-the-max government programs.

Source: David Brown, Toronto Star

THE DANGEROUS MYTH OF STOCK MARKET RISKS

History demonstrates that there is virtually no risk in the stock market as long as an investor is in it for the long haul. Those who will lose are the ones standing on the sidelines, their wealth parked in houses and GICs, and warning one day the Dow could fall 1,000 points, or maybe even 1,500. It could, and possibly will.

But smart investors knew it was not the end of the world when the equivalent happened on October 19, 1987—Black Monday. In hindsight, it turned out to be a heck of a buying opportunity, which is exactly what the next dump turned out to be 10 years later almost to the day.

Consider this. . .

$100,000 put into Templeton Growth 20 years ago grew into more than $2 million. And don't forget, during the past 20 years, our economy has endured an oil crisis, two recessions, high interest rates, soaring inflation, numerous wars, the collapse of the Soviet empire, El Nino-related natural disasters, major and minor market corrections, Bre-X, the Far East meltdown, dot-com boom and bust, and a host of other calamities.

BE AWARE THAT:

- Some real estate values may never recover to their 1980s highs.
- The long-term outlook for residential real estate is slower appreciation.
- Most residential real estate has no long-term future as an investment.
- Prices will probably decline; at best, they will remain the same.
- As real estate values decline, the value of your equity goes down, not the amount of your mortgage.
- Your home can be a valuable asset if it is managed properly.
- Canadians have too much of their personal wealth tied up in their homes.
- At least half your net worth should be assets outside of your home.
- Residential real estate is not an appropriate asset for most seniors.
- Removing net worth from your home is as easy as getting a home equity loan for investment purposes.

Chapter 8

The RRSP mortgage and other options

If you own a house, you can put your mortgage inside your RRSP, make mortgage payments to yourself, and also exceed the allowed contribution levels. It is a bit tricky, and you need to closely follow the rules.

HOW AN RRSP MORTGAGE WORKS

Your RRSP is allowed to hold a mortgage on any Canadian real estate you own—residential or commercial—or on property owned by an immediate relative. That means you can take money in your RRSP and loan it out as a mortgage. Then you make regular payments back into your RRSP. You will end up putting far more back into your RRSP than you ever took out—this is the only way to contribute more to your RRSP than is allowed by contribution rules. Here's how you make the best of it:

- Go with the longest amortization period. The longer it takes to pay off, the more interest accrues and the greater the amount of money goes into the RRSP.
- Your RRSP mortgage interest rate must be "comparable" to market rates. Shop around, find the highest rate offered commercially, and use it as your RRSP mortgage rate.
- Make your RRSP mortgage an open one, which would allow you to pay it off at any time (which you have no intention of doing). Open mortgages cost a premium rate, meaning your interest is greater.
- You can make the mortgage a second one, to boost the interest rate even higher. (But this will also cost you more in mortgage insurance—

all RRSP mortgages must be insured by Canada Mortgage and Housing Corporation (CMHC) or GE Capital.)

- Stay away from accelerated mortgage repayment methods. In other words, you want a monthly-pay mortgage, instead of a weekly one that cuts repayment time and saves interest.
- If you default, your RRSP ends up with ownership of your home— which you don't want.
- RRSPs are allowed to finance real estate, not own it. If you default, your plan will have to sell the home within a year, at market value.

HOW TO SET IT UP

There are certainly expensive set-up costs and moderate maintenance costs involved and this must be done through a self-directed retirement plan. But it's still worth it. Here's the procedure:

- Costs include an appraisal fee (typically $150 to $200), legal fees ($500 or more), and a one-time set-up fee (anywhere from $100 to $300). Also, RRSP mortgages must be insured, generally about 2% of the mortgage amount. Normally you'd pay this in cash rather than add it to the mortgage principal, because by tacking it on, it becomes amortized and ends up costing you three times what you borrowed. But in this case, the goal is to get money into your RRSP, and you'll gladly add it to the outstanding debt.
- Once in place, the RRSP mortgage has some ongoing costs. The annual fee for the self-directed plan is typically $150, and the mortgage administration fee varies from less than $100 to almost $300 annually. Canada Customs and Revenue Agency stipulates that you can't administer your own RRSP mortgage—you'll need a third-party agent, typically a trust company.
- Not all financial institutions will allow you to have an RRSP mortgage within a self-directed plan. Others will only allow it on your principal residence. Still, others are flexible—so shop around.
- You need to have enough cash or cashable assets in your RRSP to equal the mortgage you are transferring to your plan. If your RRSP assets are locked into GICs, for example, it won't work. Once the RRSP mortgage is set up, it's locked in until the time of renewal, when you have some options.

GETTING EQUITY OUT OF YOUR HOME

In cases where people have existing home mortgages and less than $50,000 cash in their RRSP, it does not make sense to set up an RRSP mortgage. Costs are too high. But there are some circumstances under which this strategy allows you to get equity out of real estate and at the same time exceed RRSP contribution levels. Do you:

- Own your home, mortgage-free, which means you have a significant amount of equity?
- Have a whack of cash or cashable assets (CSBs, strip bonds, mutual funds and so on) in your RRSP?
- Have a good cash flow that you'd like to divert into your RRSP?

Here's a plan for somebody with $150,000 equity in their home, and an equal amount in RRSP assets, invested in a 6%, five-year GIC (the typical Canadian strategy):

1. **Take out a home equity loan for $150,000**—Easily done through financial institutions. Most full-service financial advisers will set it up too.
2. **Invest that money in equity-based mutual funds to earn at least 10%**—Now your home equity loan is deemed to be an investment loan for tax purposes.
3. **The interest on the equity loan becomes tax-deductible**—So, if you are in the 54% tax bracket, at income tax time, deduct 54% of the interest paid all year.
4. **Now, set up an RRSP mortgage**—Have your retirement plan buy out the bank or trust company mortgage. You can insure this through GE Capital or, if you have waited up to a year after taking the equity loan, CMHC will insure the mortgage (CMHC has a rule against insuring equity loans, but after a certain period of time in existence it becomes a normal mortgage).

Okay, let's review: You have withdrawn $150,000 of the equity in your home and it is now earning at least 10% (instead of zero). At the same time, you have created a tax deduction and reduced your income tax load. And now your RRSP holds a $150,000 mortgage, instead of the assets that used to be there.

5. **Now, every month, you cut a mortgage payment cheque to your RRSP**—At a five-year rate of around 8% each year, you would be contributing more than $15,000 to your RRSP. That's more than the

current maximum limit of $13,500, and it doesn't matter what your income level is.

6. **In five years, you would be able to contribute more than $75,000 into your RRSP**—During that time if you put that money into growth-oriented mutual funds averaging 10%, your RRSP would have more than $100,000 returned to it.

The bottom line is increased wealth. Five years after having $150,000 equity in your home and $150,000 in your RRSP (which would have grown to just over $200,000), you'd have a total of $350,000. Instead, now you have a $150,000 mortgage in your RRSP, about $100,000 in new RRSP assets and over $200,000 in outside investments (assuming the $150,000 grew by about 12% to 13% after capital gains tax) for a total of around $450,000.

If you had not arranged the equity loan and then the RRSP mortgage, the $150,000 in your RRSP would certainly have continued to grow, but the equity in your home likely would not have grown. And you would not have had the mortgage interest to help reduce your taxable income.

THE HOME BUYERS' PLAN: BUYER BEWARE

In place for almost a decade, the Home Buyers' Plan is still popular, and provides many individuals with that extra cash needed to make the jump to home ownership. But there are perils inherent in using this plan.

How it works
Here are the basics:

- You can withdraw up to $20,000 from existing funds in your RRSP to buy a home.
- If you have a spouse, together you can withdraw up to $40,000.
- The plan is open only to first-time buyers.
- You must be a Canadian resident with an RRSP who has not used this plan before.
- You must not have owned a home in the last five years, or be married to or living with someone (of the opposite sex) who has owned in the last five years.
- You must buy an existing or to-be-built house by October 1 of the year following the withdrawal.

- It can be a condo, detached home, mobile trailer, apartment unit in a duplex or triplex, co-operative or townhouse.
- The money can't be used to pay down an existing mortgage or fix up a house that you already own.
- To apply, simply fill out the right form at your bank or trust company and then withdraw the money from your RRSP. No taxes will be withheld.

In effect, you are taking an interest-free loan from your RRSP, which you will have to pay back. Miss a repayment, and it becomes part of your income that year, and that means you pay tax on it, and lose the ability to put it back into your RRSP.

How you repay the interest-free loan

You must repay the money in equal payments within 15 years of withdrawing it—$1,333 annually on $20,000. Repayment starts in the second calendar year after you borrow. A loan taken in 2001 will need repayment in 2003. But that can be delayed. Repayment rules were changed to the RRSP contribution deadline—60 days into the next year. Borrow in 2001 and your first payment is due March 1, 2004.

Repayments do not have to be made into the same RRSP they came out of but you can't claim a tax deduction on a repayment—you received that deduction when the money first went in.

CCRA will send you notification forms giving an annual statement and it will:

- Tell you exactly how much is due, and by when.
- Provide a summary of payments made. You can pay more than required, but not less.

When you make an overpayment, future payments will be scaled back to reflect that, and if you are turning 69 and your plan isn't paid back, you can pay it out in full if you have the money, or include it in your income each year, and spread the tax liability out.

A neat strategy to use

If you are planning to buy a home, and you don't have an RRSP, try and make the closing date on the real estate transaction 90 days or more from the time of signing the offer. This way you can make an RRSP contribution and take out a tax-free, interest-free loan under the

Home Buyers' Plan in the same year. The two actions just have to be at least 90 days apart. Here's how:

- Go to the bank, trust company or personal adviser and open an RRSP.
- Withdraw $20,000 from your down-payment savings and put it in your RRSP if you have the room.
- From that you will earn a tax rebate cheque of $8,000 if you're in the 40% tax bracket.
- On closing 90 days later, use the Home Buyers' Plan to withdraw the $20,000, without penalty.
- Now you have increased your wealth by $8,000 in three months, by filling out two forms.
- For first-time home buyers, $8,000 extra can sure come in handy.

The plan can also be dangerous

The point of RRSPs is to encourage people to save for their retirement. The Home Buyers' Plan was intended to be a temporary stimulus to the real estate industry during the 1990s recession. But since it has become permanent, it represents a serious precedent for using the $150-billion RRSP pot for things other than retirement.

Consider this. There is no way your house value will grow in the next three decades to compensate for the lost power of that $20,000 growing tax-free within your RRSP. And the younger you are, the more money you will lose.

> ## Did you know. . .
> . . . that $20,000 withdrawn from an RRSP in your twenties can represent $200,000 lost when you are in your sixties? Will your home rise 10 times in value by 2037? If it paces inflation, you'll be doing well.

Think hard before you remove RRSP money for a down payment. If you decide to borrow, repay it quickly—don't spread it out over a long 15 years. And certainly keep putting money into your RRSP after you buy the house.

KEEP THIS IN MIND:

- Your RRSP can hold your mortgage.
- You must have cash or cashable assets in your RRSP equal to the mortgage.
- Because of associated costs, this strategy works best for amounts substantially above $50,000.
- You can end up putting more into your RRSP than you withdrew.
- You can even exceed contribution limits by holding an RRSP mortgage.
- First-time home buyers can tap their RRSP for an interest-free loan—up to $20,000.
- If you have a spouse, together you can take out a tax-free loan for up to $40,000.
- Repayment—in equal installments—must be made within 15 years of taking out the loan.
- You are losing the tax-free compounding of that money during the time it is outside your RRSP.

Chapter 9

Top 10 strategies you can't afford to ignore

The new millennium is a critical point for most Canadians. The economy and financial markets have made fantastic strides since the recession of the early 1990s yet most people are not investing smartly.

How can you take advantage? Follow along:

- Study the strategies I am presenting in this book.
- Discuss them with your financial adviser.
- If you don't have an adviser, get one.
- Do what most Canadians will not—take action and implement these strategies.
- Never assume that in the years to come the government will support you, or that future investments will make up for lost ground.

Did you know. . .

. . .there is nothing weak about the economy—the economic future is bright? The problem is that Canadians are investing in the wrong ways, in the wrong places. Too few are taking advantage of today's outstanding opportunities. Worse, they are not harnessing the power of the RRSP.

Most Canadians, especially boomers, are still wedded to the twin myths that:

1. Retirement assets should be held in risk-free investments.
2. Money ploughed into real estate is safe.

Individuals who do not quickly shake those beliefs will end up both bitter and poorer. Don't be one of them. So let's begin. . . .

1. GO FOR GROWTH

RRSPs are merely mechanisms for shielding your assets from tax—ideal for harbouring highly taxed assets such as strip bonds. For example, a government bond held within an RRSP would give you double the return on the same bond held outside the plan—even assuming that you paid the top marginal tax rate when you cashed out the RRSP.

Consider this. . .

An RRSP is so effective at maximizing the yield on strip bond investment that—according to Bruce Cohen of the *Financial Post*—future tax rates could soar as high as 82% and you'd still be better off having money in an RRSP cashed out at that tax level.

Assets that are most susceptible to tax should go into your RRSP first

That includes strip bonds, savings bonds, mortgages and GICs. Growth investments, even with a lower tax profile than bonds and investment certificates, also belong in your RRSP. It is essential to have growth-oriented assets in your plan. And the best growth assets are stocks and mutual funds. Quality, equity-based mutual funds have been giving investors double-digit returns for most of the last decade.

Some people worry that with so much money on the move, another huge stock-market correction is imminent and we could head into a 1929-style crash. But with an aging North American population, the need for high rates of return will likely keep most investors in the market and even increase their holdings when prices take the inevitable tumble.

Make sure you grab some of this growth. I fail to see the risk in buying and holding quality funds as long as you are a long-term investor—a minimum of five years. Fifteen years would be even better.

As a matter of fact. . .

. . .if you take a look at any chart of the stock market over 15, 40 or 100 years, you can clearly see that the trend for prices is higher. Smart money buys on weakness and only sells on necessity, not panic.

Over the last three decades, the Toronto Stock Exchange has yielded an average of almost 10%—beating out every other asset class. In 1999 it advanced 32%. And now with low inflation and interest rates, equities will attract more interest and the pressure for higher prices will increase. Can you afford not to invest?

2. MAKE THOSE MISSED CONTRIBUTIONS—NOW

The RRSP is the best tax shelter in North America, so it's a shock that less than a third of the people who file tax returns make an RRSP contribution. And that's not all:

- Only 11% make their maximum contributions.
- Millions of people have savings that are not tax-sheltered in an RRSP.
- Others don't realize that a $100 monthly contribution can result in a $250,000 RRSP in 25 years.
- Total unused contribution room is mushrooming, nearing the point where it may never be realized.

And there is no reason to believe that this huge amount of contribution room exists because people don't know any better. A study published by the Bank of Nova Scotia found that 87% of Canadians know they can make up missed contributions. Equally disturbing: more than half of those surveyed hadn't a clue how much room they had to work with, or where they could get this information.

If you are reading this book during "RRSP season"—those few weeks of the year prior to the beginning of March—then this is what I want you to do:

1. Make your full 2000 contribution.

2. Make the allowable overcontribution of $2,000.

3. Catch up on all of your missed past contributions.

4. Go to your bank, trust, broker or adviser's office. Open a self-directed RRSP and fill it up, investing in a mix of stocks, bonds and mutual funds that suits your goals. Make sure 25% of it is foreign content. And, if you don't have that much extra money, borrow it. If you deal with a financial adviser, in many cases he or she has access to capital at even cheaper rates than the banks or trust companies.

Usually you won't have to start repayment until you receive your tax refund, which should be used to pay down part of the loan.

3. CONTRIBUTE AT THE RIGHT TIME

Every year people make the same mistake. They contribute to an RRSP exactly 12 to 14 months later than they should have. The rules say we all have until 60 days after the end of a taxation year to make a contribution that can be used to reduce taxes in that year.

Sure, it is a good thing to put money into a plan at any time, but by always making that contribution at the very end of the allowable period, instead of at the beginning, you lose an entire year in which that money could have been growing tax-free.

Consider this. . .
By putting $3,500 in at the beginning of the year, instead of at the end, a mutual fund earning 10% will give you almost $60,000 more after 30 years. That, of course, is money for nothing—no additional contribution. No borrowing. No pain. No risk. All you have done is change the day on which you made the contribution.

By all means, contribute to your RRSP early in the year, but do it a year early. And you can also get on a monthly plan to have RRSP money debited from your paycheque or chequing account on a regular basis.

4. MAX YOUR CASH FLOW

No money left at the end of the month to put towards retirement? No problem, we can fix that using this strategy. Most middle-class people work for paycheques. Federal and provincial income taxes are deducted from those cheques. Follow along and see how that amount can be reduced.

The key is to make your RRSP contribution either at the beginning of the taxation year, or in monthly installments. This way you increase your cash flow by reducing your paycheque taxes instead of waiting a year for that refund cheque. Here's what to do:

- Make your yearly contribution in January (14 months ahead of the actual deadline); borrow the money if necessary.
- Set up monthly RRSP contributions, using preauthorized chequing-account withdrawals.
- Call the local CCRA district taxation office and ask for the phone number of Source Deductions.
- Call Source Deductions and tell them that you want your withholding tax adjusted for RRSP contributions. Inform them that you want a Tax Deduction Waiver. They'll ask for your estimated income for this year, expected deductions and you must provide proof of RRSP contribution.
- CCRA will consider this, and then, when approved, will send the waiver to your employer, who will reduce the tax taken off your cheque. It will take about a month, and you will have to do this annually.

Don't squander your fatter paycheque on incidentals. You could:

- Take that money and simply increase your mortgage payments, shortening the time before it's completely paid off (and then replace it with a tax-deductible investment mortgage).
- Or, purchase mutual fund units on a monthly basis, again through preauthorized debits.

The bottom line here is pretty simple: either you are a serious, long-term, dedicated RRSP contributor, or you are gambling with your future.

5. TAKE YOUR SPOUSE TO THE BANK

Even as the federal government gradually introduces tax cuts, most Canadians will still pay too much tax. Taxes are wealth killers. That is where an RRSP comes in. It can let you move as many assets as possible into the hands of the least-taxed spouse. In other words, split income.

The easiest way to split income is with spousal RRSPs. This money becomes your spouse's property, as long as it's left in the plan for three years. And your contribution to the spousal plan doesn't prevent your spouse from also contributing to a separate personal plan. You don't even need to be married—common-law is okay, but to date, you do have to be of the opposite sex.

A fact of life. . .

. . . is that seniors are sitting ducks for increased government taxation—especially well-off seniors who, ironically, were the ones who prepared for retirement. Clawbacks of pension benefits will only increase. The best defence is to even out income flow between you and your spouse. Start doing that now, no matter how far off retirement is.

For example, if a couple were each able to withdraw $28,000 income from retirement plans, instead of one spouse taking $56,000, they'd pay 10% less income tax and give up far fewer pension benefits. Unfortunately, many of today's retired Canadians are in the unhappy position of having virtually all family income flow through the hands of one spouse.

You can avoid that situation. Spousal RRSPs are one way to do this. Paying your less-taxed spouse's taxes are another. Or pay your spouse or children a salary. You can also bankroll a spouse's business so that profits are attributed to him or her, not you.

6. MAKE THAT OVERCONTRIBUTION

You are allowed to contribute up to $2,000 more into your plan than the rules normally allow. Do it now for several reasons:

- It's hard enough getting enough money into your RRSP where it grows tax-free, so even though you don't receive a tax break for the overcontribution, it's still worth sheltering the money.
- Carrying around an extra $2,000 in your RRSP is a good idea. Should you get laid off or lose your job, and don't have enough earned income to make an RRSP contribution next year, you can use that money instead, and you will also receive a deduction on your taxes.
- If you have a dependant aged 19 or older, make the overcontribution in his or her name if the child does not have earned income and can't contribute to his or her own plan. There's no tax deduction, but when your child reaches age 59, the $2,000 could be worth $90,000.
- If you are retired but still have earned income (such as from a rental house), make the overcontribution. As long as you continue to have

earned income, you can claim the deduction yearly at the rate of 18% of income, until the $2,000 is exhausted. The same applies to a spousal plan.

7. GET A LOAN WITH NO INTEREST

This is a strategy only for first-time homebuyers who can withdraw up to $20,000 each ($40,000 for a couple) to use as a down payment on a home—either new or resale.

It is, in effect, an interest-free and tax-free loan from your RRSP, and must be repaid in equal installments over 15 years. Miss a payment and it becomes taxable as part of your income in that year. You have at least two years before repayment must start. If you can manage a down payment without help from your RRSP, keep your money working in it. If not, here's a way to use the money and then some:

- If you are a couple in the 40% tax bracket with $20,000 saved for a down payment, plus missed RRSP contributions, make those contributions now.
- Go house-hunting, but do not close a deal prior to 90 days after you made the RRSP contribution.
- Cash in the RRSPs, tax-free under the Home Buyers' Plan.
- Add to that the $8,000 Ottawa sent you in tax refunds because you contributed to your RRSP (which you actually spent on a house). Now you have $28,000 to put down, and a smaller mortgage.
- The $20,000 will have to be paid back into your RRSP, starting in the year 2003 at the rate of $1,300 a year. If you can do it faster, it's to your benefit.

As a matter of fact. . .

. . .if you withdraw $5,000 from your RRSP 30 years before retirement, and that amount was compounding annually at 10%, you could end up with $85,000 less savings in your golden years. And there's no way you can get that $5,000 back in later when you're flush. Be wary of resorting to RRSP withdrawals if you need money—exhaust all other options first.

8. NO CASH? NO PROBLEM

You don't need money to make an RRSP contribution. All you need are some assets. The government will pay you for selling yourself what you already own. You can move assets that are currently subject to tax into your tax-free RRSP, to the limit of your annual contribution, and then claim this as a tax deduction.

It's called "contributions in kind," and it's a terrific way for people to catch up on retirement savings. It's also a strategy that every investor should use to reduce the tax load. Here's an example of a person with $7,000 in savings bonds but no RRSP. Let's turn $7,000 into $39,000. Here's how:

- Open a self-directed RRSP.
- Transfer the bonds into the plan and cash them.
- Borrow $2,800 from the bank; pay it off a full two months later with the tax refund for transferring the CBSs into the RRSP.
- Now there's enough in the RRSP to purchase a Government of Ontario strip bond with a maturity value of $39,000. It can be held to maturity or sold off earlier for a capital gain if interest rates drop.

9. HOLD YOUR OWN MORTGAGE

As outlined in the previous chapter, it is possible to put your own residential mortgage inside your RRSP and make mortgage payments to yourself. It amounts to a regular, forced transfer of wealth from your income stream into your RRSP. By setting it up properly, you can exceed your annual allowed contribution limits. The process is a bit complicated though. You will need:

- The help of a competent financial adviser
- Money—about $1,000—to set it up, and several hundred dollars a year to administer it
- A lot of cash, or cashable investments, in your RRSP—enough to write a new mortgage that will replace the one already in place
- A self-directed RRSP; it will lend enough money to discharge the existing mortgage, replace it with a new one, and take title to the property
- To have the mortgage insured

- An unrelated lender (typically a trust company) to administer it
- A lawyer, as usual

Once that is in place, you make regular mortgage payments every month into your RRSP. CCRA dictates that the mortgage rate must be comparable with existing current rates. You can't issue yourself a 2% home loan, but you wouldn't want to do that anyway because you want to give yourself the highest possible mortgage rate—because the idea is to use this device to squeeze as much of your income as possible into the RRSP.

This is not a device for making real estate more affordable. Instead, it's a strategy to bloat your retirement savings. Follow the rules carefully, or CCRA will disqualify the deal and your taxes will throb.

The bottom line, however, is that this is very much worth doing as an aggressive RRSP strategy. And it makes even more sense when your RRSP lends out money to finance an income-generating property such as a rental house. Then the interest payments you are making into your own RRSP are deductible from your taxable income. Heard of double taxation? This is the opposite.

10. PUT YOUR HOUSE TO WORK

In the first half of your life, it makes sense to acquire and pay off real estate. In the second half, use your real estate as a tool to gain more financial assets or as a source of equity to invest in financial assets. Your RRSP can help.

If you have a paid-up, mortgage-free home, then it represents a lot of money—often hundreds of thousands of dollars—typically earning peanuts in capital appreciation. At least a portion of this money could, and should, be out working in the global economy making double-digit returns.

No matter how much equity you have in your home, will that value double every five or six years? Hardly likely. But if you take out a loan against that value, or part of it, and invest the money in quality stocks and mutual funds, you could easily double your investment in a five- or six-year period. And the interest you would pay on that loan would be tax-deductible (another saving) because the money is being used for investment purposes. You'll be so much further ahead, and you'll still own your home.

Did you know. . .

. . .it pays off handsomely to remortgage a home? By investing the money in mutual funds, you can create a tax-deductible mortgage. Because the proceeds of the mortgage are used to buy financial assets yielding a greater return than the cost of the mortgage, you get to write off the interest payments from your taxable income. In tax terms, it's considered not to be a mortgage, but an investment loan. But it sure looks and smells like a mortgage to your RRSP.

Chapter 10

Living with the Bloc and other Canadian realities

I f you can use any or all of the 10 strategies presented in the previous chapter, you're well on your way to financial security. Here are a few more strategies, along with a few words of caution that, if heeded, will pay off nicely.

LUCIEN BOUCHARD AND YOUR WEALTH

Sovereignty. The rhetoric still flares up occasionally, but for the past couple of years, things have been rather quiet. Popular support in Quebec for separation is nowhere near as high as it once was, and there's a general dissatisfaction with the PQ government. For now.

The PQ almost won the last referendum, and terrified investors dumped millions of dollars in stock and bond funds in the weeks running up to the vote. The next day, when financial markets rallied dramatically, all those people who had sold decided to buy back again. How typically Canadian. Wait for a crisis, sell low and then buy high. Panicked, knee-jerk investing. And it just about guarantees that you will lose money. But there is a way to partially protect yourself from similar situations, and that is to ensure that you are completely topped up on foreign content in your RRSP (as outlined in Chapter 5).

GETTING THAT EDGE

A study conducted a couple of years ago by Environics for the Royal Bank showed that foreign investment and wealth go hand in hand. Among the country's top 10% by income, 68% own some form of global investments. In sharp contrast, while almost 70% of wealthy people have international investments, just 28% of all Canadians

"So, as you can see, since the merger, we've wasted no time Canadianizing our operation."

Source: David Brown, Toronto Star

polled by a Royal Trust survey intended to put RRSP money into foreign holdings.

The rules allow you to have 25% of your total RRSP book value in foreign content. The Canadian dollar has eroded steadily in recent years. With the Quebec situation unresolved, the possibility of another referendum, and with Canada still doing little to resolve its debt, the loonie is always at risk.

Now is the time to be prudent:

- Review your portfolio with a financial adviser.
- Buy a government or corporate bond that pays in yen if you like fixed-income investments.
- Buy shares in one of the banks, and go for preferreds that give dividends in U.S. dollars.
- Seek out and invest in Canadian companies that earn most of their income offshore.

Actions like these will help preserve your wealth when separation talk eventually resurfaces.

DO IT NOW, ENJOY IT LATER

This strategy allows people who know they will be earning more money later to maximize their tax savings. If you know your earnings will rise, make the RRSP contribution today but save the official tax receipt for later. There is nothing in the rules that says the receipt must be attached to the annual tax return for the year in which the contribution was made.

This works well for a salesperson in a cyclical industry (such as real estate), who wants to keep making RRSP contributions. Just save up the receipts to offset income earned in a good year. It also works for a graduating professional just starting to build a practice, or a high-salaried woman on maternity leave.

In these instances the tax receipt will actually be worth more in tax savings later—so why not wait? Just keep good records and don't lose the receipts.

MIX IT UP

"Don't put all your eggs into one basket." Wise investors know that. Diversification is the great equalizer when it comes to market volatility. Failing to adequately mix up your portfolio is not the biggest stumble you can make. The greatest mistake Canadian investors make is doing their own financial planning. The second mistake flows out of the first because most of us are wimps—and we attempt to avoid all risk when it comes to investing, settling mostly for GICs—the worst investment you can make.

Did you know. . .

. . .that almost half of all retired Canadians, according to Statistics Canada, are living on less than $15,000 annual personal income? The maximum benefits provided by OAS and CPP are around $4,847 and $8,937 respectively. Don't count on that increasing in the future.

Most Canadians have no idea that few investments are safer over the long haul than the stock market. Yes, there are periods of volatility after stock values rise too quickly, but those should simply be viewed as buying opportunities.

Most Canadians do not realize that stock values reflect technological advance, medical breakthroughs and economic expansion. If you have any faith in the future, then equities are the place to be. Just remember to buy quality stocks and mutual funds.

But beware of "hot" stocks—ones that receive headline attention because they soar in value, making early investors rich (remember Bre-X and Bid.com). The odds are against them. That's not investing, that's a crapshoot. Remember these rules:

- Hot stocks get cold real fast. By the time the newspapers notice a flaming stock, it has already peaked.
- If you want to play, watch what stock promoters and insiders are doing with their holdings. When they start to bail, go with them.
- And never put all your financial resources into one play—5% to 10% of your portfolio's worth will give you a good return if the stock soars. If it doesn't, you won't suffer an irreversible setback.
- You are always better to diversify. Don't invest in one stock; invest in ten. Don't invest in just one sector of the economy, but several.
- The best diversification comes via mutual funds—you buy less risk along with superior management. Don't diversify too much, or you can water down returns. Eight or nine funds will get the job done.
- Buy companies with proven track records. Your financial adviser and the Internet are excellent resources for performance data.
- Increase your holdings when stock values fall. Corrections are inevitable. They terrify many novice market players but pose huge buying opportunities for long-term investors.

Usually, stocks that pay dividends or capital gains should be held outside your RRSP. That way you don't lose the benefit of the dividend tax credit or more favourable treatment of capital gains. This holds true for those with substantial assets. But most people don't have the wealth to justify two separate portfolios, so they should concentrate on building their RRSP with diversified holdings.

Even beyond the age of 65, investors must have a strong growth component to their retirement savings because the odds of living another 25 years are improving every day.

> ## As a matter of fact. . .
> . . .don't forget what history shows us—there is no risk in the market for long-term investors. The market will continue to rise as humankind continues to advance. I can't find any evidence that a decline has begun.

THE PAIN OF LABOUR FUNDS

Five years ago, it looked as though it was impossible to lose making an RRSP investment in a labour-sponsored venture capital fund. After all, the tax incentives were almost unbelievable. The labour funds were given this amazingly favourable treatment to encourage the growth of pools of capital that would flow out into the economy, into small and medium-sized enterprises, creating jobs. Nice theory.

Investors gorged on these things, pumping in millions of dollars until the total pot stood at about $2 billion. However, like a lot of theories, once they're off the drawing board, it becomes evident they are exactly that—nice theories. Many funds have been unable to find companies to invest in. Others have non-existent or poor track records. Too many investors asked too few questions, caring only about the tax savings. As a result, they ended up with bad investments.

Are labour funds a good investment? Not any more. At least, not most of them. The main reason is that shortly after the 1996 RRSP season, all the rules changed. The main changes came a year or so ago when Finance Minister Paul Martin announced the following:

- The federal tax credit was being reduced from 20% to 15%.
- The maximum share purchase eligible for the tax credit was being reduced from $5,000 to $3,500.
- The minimum holding period for labour fund shares was being increased from five to eight years, including for seniors and retirees. In Quebec, in most cases, investors must hold the money in a fund until retirement.
- The ability to double-dip has ended. Investors can no longer redeem shares at the end of the holding period and then immediately reinvest the money to receive a new set of tax credits. Now, an investor must wait two years past the year of redemption before being able to reinvest and receive a tax break.

SHIELD YOUR WEALTH FROM CREDITORS

Most people are shocked to learn that federal law does not protect RRSP assets from creditors. In fact, your investment can be at risk in several ways:

- If your marriage breaks up, provincial law allows your ex-spouse to make a claim against your RRSP assets. In general, you will lose half.
- If the financial institution holding your RRSP goes belly-up, as Confederation Life did, you lose all assets beyond the insured limit of $60,000 for cash, GIC, term deposits and so on.
- If you die owing CCRA money for unpaid taxes, your RRSP can be opened under the Income Tax Act, allowing the feds to get their money.
- If you go bankrupt, creditors could get a court order against your RRSP if the money you put in there over the last few years could have been used to pay off bills.

You can increase protection from creditors by naming your spouse as the beneficiary of your retirement plan. This step also allows the transfer of the RRSP assets upon death to the spouse, and avoids probate fees.

If you think you'll have problems with creditors in the future, use a spousal RRSP to harbour your assets (as long as your spouse isn't on the lam from the law). Assets put into a spousal plan become the possessions of your spouse. RRSPs with life insurance companies are also protected from creditors.

Losing anything over the $60,000 liability limit for cash, GICs and term deposits with a financial institution that fails, makes a strong point for adjusting your portfolio. One way to protect yourself is to convert some or all of these interest-bearing investments into quality mutual funds. Mutual funds are not owned by the financial institution or investment house, but held in trust on your behalf by a bank or trust company.

DON'T FOLLOW THE HERD

The most important thing you can do when investing your RRSP money is to ensure that you maintain a long-term view. The shift away from real assets, including real estate, will only continue as the North

American population ages. Billions of dollars will flow into equities and funds for more than a decade, pushing valuations higher. More and more people will wake up to the fact that the single best strategy is for them to drain out the equity in their homes while financial institutions are still offering home equity loans.

In the future, selling a suburban house could be simply impossible. So now is the time for middle-aged investors to cash out real estate, or at least to use its equity to acquire financial assets.

Did you know. . .

. . .it took the Dow 44 years to hit the 1000-point mark? It took just 25 years more to crack 8000, and only 189 trading days for the Dow to vault from 8000 to 9000 points.

But will those financial assets—stocks, bonds, mutual funds—tank in the future in the same way most real estate did in the past decade? Anything is possible, but it's unlikely unless, in the decades to come, there's a bout of hyper-inflation triggered by a debt crisis or a major international armed conflict. In circumstances like those, people with their wealth in oil and gold would win. In any case, unwavering demographics would still dictate tough times for real estate, which dances only to one beat: supply and demand.

WHY BUY A GIC WHEN THERE ARE STRIP BONDS?

Canadians with any of their RRSP assets in GICs are making a big mistake—interest rates are low, the investment is locked up for years, and there's no potential of a capital gain. Why would anyone put their money in a GIC? They think it's safe. Well, there is an even safer place for retirement money that offers huge advantages over a GIC: strip bonds. These investment products:

- Pay more interest
- Are cashable anytime
- Are free of risk—there is no limit similar to the $60,000 insurance threshold for GICs

- Increase in value when interest rates decrease, giving a capital gain
- Can be purchased at a deep discount to face value
- And when safely tucked into your self-directed RRSP, they are virtual money machines—doubling or tripling your investment in a defined period of time.

Why doesn't everyone have strips? Because they don't sell them at most banks, and so most people are unaware of the strip bond alternative. Do not confuse these with Canada Savings Bonds or provincial copycats such as Ontario Savings Bonds—tepid investments scarcely better than GICs.

A fact of life. . .
The greatest risk you face is not losing your money, but rather outliving it. Being content with a low-yielding GIC is false security.

No, real government bonds are different, but as accessible as one phone call to your independent financial adviser. Categorized as "fixed income," these bonds pay a predetermined amount of interest when held to maturity. But, unlike GICs and CSBs, strip bonds fluctuate in value daily, rising or falling in reverse to interest rates, and they can be bought or sold at any time, no matter what maturity date they carry.

SO, WHAT IS A GOVERNMENT STRIP BOND?

Basically it's a regular government bond issued by any Canadian province, or other bodies such as Ontario Power Generation, as part of the ongoing process of financing government spending. Regular bonds pay investors interest, usually twice a year (some pay monthly), so they are good for people looking for a steady, guaranteed income.

But brokers can take the bonds and separate them into two—the interest coupons and the principal. You can buy either the coupons, which will then give you income on a regular basis but no pay-out at the end. Or, you can buy the bond itself (which is stripped of interest—giving rise to the term "strip" bond), which will pay you face value on the day of maturity, or whatever the market value is on whatever day prior to maturity on which you decide to sell.

Strip bonds are also issued by corporations, but are not as secure as government strips because they're backed by corporate assets, not the power of taxation. And that power to tax is exactly what gives strip bonds their security. It's as close to a complete guarantee as you will ever get.

Consider this. . .

If the government ever defaulted on a bond issue, that would pretty well be the end of the Canadian dollar—including the ones in your GIC. In such a case you could almost certainly forget about the Canada Deposit Insurance Corporation refunding your money. It would be swept away in an instant.

Because the strip bond pays no interest, you buy it at a big discount to its face value. That means you can leverage a big pay-out years later with a much smaller amount of money now. The longer the period until the bond matures, the bigger the discount. And the higher the yield on the bond, the cheaper it is to buy.

Government bonds come in maturities ranging from six months to 30 years. Shorter-term, mini-bonds are called Treasury bills (T-bills), also backed by the power to tax and available in terms of 30, 60, 90 or 180 days. They're a good place to park cash for a while.

Some investment firms will "package" together a number of bonds of various types and maturities specifically for RRSPs. Many of these offerings are excellent, and just having access to them alone is worth the effort of finding a good, independent financial adviser.

Now, strip bonds are wonderful RRSP instruments, and every portfolio should have some. But make sure your asset mix is right—and that bonds are held alongside equities and mutual funds.

Outside an RRSP, strips are less attractive as CCRA will tax you on interest income not yet received. That's the same negative tax situation as a GIC or CSB—so all should properly be tax-sheltered.

STRIPS AND LADDERS

Here's a risk-free, long-term investment and retirement strategy you just can't beat. Because strip bonds are purchased at a discount to face value, the longer until a bond matures, the cheaper it is to buy.

For example: When my mother was 81 (I am forbidden from revealing her current age), she wanted to leave some money for educating a grandchild—money not needed for 15 years. She could have set aside $8,000 from her estate. Or, she could spend the money on a cruise and use just a portion of it to buy a strip bond that would accomplish the same purpose.

So she did. She bought a strip maturing in 2010 that would be worth $8,000. For each $100 of the bond, she paid just $24.88, so the total cost of buying the bond was $1,999. And the interest that will end up in the hands of the grandchild is $6,000, plus the bond purchase price.

Action Plan Requirement. . .
Every boomer should assemble a ladder of strip bonds with staggered maturity dates to ensure a cash stream in the future. As each bond matures, the money can be spent on more strips to keep the ladder going. Once in place, the effect of compounding interest is awesome.

Imagine if you expanded on what my mother did. If, for the next 15 years, you put your annual RRSP contribution into a strip bond with a 15-year maturity, then every year, starting in 2015 and lasting until 2030, you'd have money coming due as retirement income.

How much? That depends on the future direction of interest rates. But if we used my mother's example, paying $24.88 for every $100 in maturity value, a $10,000 RRSP contribution made today will ensure a return of $40,192 in 15 years. Yes, that's guaranteed.

Or you can purchase a number of strip bonds with varying maturity dates, with money you may now have inside your RRSP, to get a maturity ladder in place right away.

So, boomers now in their forties and fifties can plan for stable retirement income by purchasing strip bonds with maturities of 15, 20 or even 30 years. That will mean receiving four to six dollars in the future for every one invested now. Using a maturity ladder you can leverage each year's allowable RRSP contribution into one more year of financial security decades from now.

WHEN YOU GOTTA GO. . .

Let's face it, we live in a country envied by many the world over. Studies conducted by the United Nations consistently cite Canada at the top of the list when it comes to a place in which to live peacefully, productively and prosperously. So who would want to leave? Well at times, you have to.

Whether it's pursuing a career abroad for a few years or snapping the old snow shovel in half and retiring to a warmer clime, you should discuss any move with your financial adviser.

For example, if you are retiring to the United States, do not withdraw a lump sum from your RRSP before heading south. Why? Well, consider these factors:

• It will trigger a big tax bite (up to 50% in the highest marginal tax bracket).
• Wait until you've given up your Canadian residency.
• Once you are a resident of the United States or any other country, the most tax CCRA will demand is a 25% withholding tax on any withdrawals. That rate drops to 15% on periodic withdrawals as opposed to lump-sum withdrawals.

On taking up residency status down south, you should also ensure that you minimize tax paid to the IRS. This involves stepping up the cost base of your assets; in other words, your book value. This can be done without adding any more money to your RRSP, and should be undertaken before assuming U.S. residency.

If your current assets' market value is, say $500,000, and this has grown from your book value of $100,000 (the original purchase price), just sell your assets and reinvest the $500,000 (even in the same investments). Now your book value is $500,000, and you can withdraw that entire amount without paying tax in the U.S. Because this strategy of increasing the cost base is conducted inside your RRSP, you will not face a tax bill from Ottawa. However, you will probably face some cost in terms of commissions.

Also, the U.S. Securities and Exchange Commission has begun cracking down on individuals managing their RRSPs—American law frowns upon resident investors buying or trading securities that are not registered in the U.S. As a Canadian investor living stateside, you can continue to hold your funds without making changes, or the option is to redeem. You could also:

- Provide a trusted individual with power of attorney to make decisions on your behalf north of the 49th.
- Another option is to dump your money into an asset-allocation program before heading to the U.S.; that way you're not required to make any decisions.
- You could also make the odd trip back to the frigid north to conduct your business, but that could end up upsetting the folks at the SEC.

Again, a thorough discussion with your accountant and financial planner can ensure that you maximize advantageous strategies when taking off.

HIGHLY RECOMMENDED ACTIONS:

- Max out your RRSP foreign-content limit to offset the fluctuating loonie.
- Make your annual contribution but save the receipt for next year if you believe you'll be earning more.
- Diversify your portfolio but stay away from so-called "hot stocks."
- Be cautious about investing in labour-sponsored funds; get some advice.
- Make sure you've done all that's possible to protect your RRSP assets from creditors.
- Don't follow the traditional approach to investing; adapt to today's new reality—financial assets.
- Forget GICs and take a look at the flexibility, solid returns and minimal risk of strip bonds.
- When leaving to reside in another country, get professional advice and avoid big tax headaches.

Preparation for every generation!

There is no one-kind-fits-all investment strategy for successful retirement planning. Even so, most Canadians believe in the same scenario: get married, buy a house, pay it off, invest in risk-free RRSP assets such as bonds and GICs, sell the house for big bucks, move into a condo and spend six months of each year being irradiated in Florida. If life were only that simple.

Unfortunately there are some giant flaws in that plan:

- Real estate has a limited future.
- The return on "safe" traditional retirement assets—bonds and GICs—is too low to keep pace with increased longevity.
- Your marriage has a fifty-fifty chance of dissolving, meaning family retirement assets may be carved in half.
- Canada Pension Plan is shaky; baby boomers may never see a government cheque in old age.
- Gen Xers are likely destined to pay more taxes for a less certain future than the self-absorbed boomers.

Despite all these obstacles, the future—at least the next 15 years— will be wonderful for those who adopt the right investment strategies, no matter what age demographic they belong to. Here are four reasons:

1. Financial markets will sparkle; cost of living will stay low.

2. Technology will continue to create unheard-of new opportunities.

3. Interest rates will stay on a low plateau.

4. Financial assets could double every 60 months without significant risk.

But you've got to know what to do, and when to do it. Now, more than ever, investment strategies must be appropriate to your age. Here are my basic suggestions:

GEN XERS

You have not been dealt a fair hand, but make the most of it. Expect higher taxes and a declining economy starting sometime after 2015. Things will get ugly for the same reason they are now streaking higher—demographics. The current North American economy will be robust for the next 15 years, but with millions of 60-year-olds around, economic growth could flame out fast.

Here's what Gen Xers must do:

1. **Maximize RRSPs**—Catch up on missed contributions even if you have to borrow. Make the $2,000 overcontribution. Income-split with your spouse as a long-term hedge against job loss.

2. **Pursue high-growth investments**—Equities and equity-based mutual funds are the only place to be. The Dow and the TSE 300 will go higher over the next few years—this is your best chance to build significant wealth quickly.

3. **Be aggressive**—Recognize obvious opportunities. Technology stocks will soar in value and an aging population will require far more health care than the public system can deliver. Wise investors will put money into nursing and retirement home companies, medical care providers, biotech firms, and so on.

4. **Adopt a sensible real estate strategy**—Now is an excellent time for first-time home buyers. Stabilized housing costs will allow you to build up financial assets more quickly, and provide some equity. But real estate could collapse within 15 years. Buy a house that you can see yourself living in for a long time.

THE BOOMERS

Boomers are in terrible shape, having saved just about 5% of what will be needed to finance retirement. Within 30 years—when the average baby boomer is 75—the number of retired people will have surged 142% while the entire Canadian population will have grown just 15%. Imagine the pressures that will put on the economy (and on health care).

Demographics are no longer on your side. Boomers will overwhelm the pension system and bankrupt public health care. If you want a happy, prosperous retirement, then you will have to earn it. Do not expect a dollar in government pensions. And expect to pay a substantial amount for adequate medical care.

Did you know. . .
. . .according to Statistics Canada, most Canadians can be expected to live for almost another 20 years beyond 65? And only half of that time will they be free of any disability.

This reality dictates an aggressive investment and tax strategy for the next 15 to 20 years. You can do it even if you are 45 and have saved nothing. You can be ready. Here's how:

- You cannot afford to miss a single RRSP contribution.
- You must reduce your tax profile by every means possible.
- You must achieve double-digit rates of return on your investments.
- You cannot afford to invest in a GIC or savings bond.
- You must raise your tolerance for risk.
- You must reconsider your real estate assets.

Fortunately for all baby boomers, you can dodge the demographic bullet, due to the incredible convergence of low inflation, falling rates and rising financial markets. This is the great second chance. Here's how to start:

1. **Baby boomers can no longer be savers**—Invest more aggressively in stocks, bonds and mutual funds, especially equity funds. There is more risk and volatility, but buy and hold quality investments, ride out fluctuations, and increase your wealth in a way not possible with GICs, CSBs, and so on.

2. **Catch up on missed RRSP contributions**—This includes the $2,000 overcontribution. Borrow if necessary.

3. **Use self-directed RRSPs**—Give yourself maximum investment flexibility. Don't be talked into a GIC-type RRSP.

4. **Invest for growth**—Boomers must be at least 75% invested in stocks or equity-based mutual funds. You need double-digit rates of return to grow the average boomer RRSP of $30,000 into at least $500,000 by 2015.

5. **Find better alternatives to GICs**—You can acquire assets with a better return than GICs. Wait until your GICs mature, cash them in, and invest in government bonds. You get a greater rate of return, the potential of a capital gain if interest rates fall further, and more security because there's no limit to the amount the government will guarantee. They're also fully cashable at any time.

Did you know. . .

. . .that the baby boomers' quest for stocks and mutual funds could power the TSE 300 to 20,000 points within the next decade? So says David Cork, author of *The Pig and the Python*. He believes that the shortage of stocks in Canada could create days that are opposite to the 1987 correction. The market could soar on a buying panic because there's an absence of sellers.

---

6. **Cash out real estate equity**—For many boomers this will be the hardest step emotionally, because we matured in an era when real estate was equated with wealth. Those days are over. In the future it will be harder to sell your home. The best thing you can do is unlock the equity in your home and get it into growth funds. You can do this by selling and downsizing to the kind of real estate that does have a future, or by taking a home equity loan and creating a tax deduction at the same time.

7. **Get professional financial help**—The greatest mistake most people make is thinking they can figure it out for themselves. Most can't. Most fail. Most believe that relying on the expertise of a financial adviser will cost a lot of money or they'll be soaked for commissions. These are dangerous myths.

8. **Hedge against the loonie**—Financial markets hate uncertainty and the dollar is at risk as long as the threat of a Quebec referendum exists. It is not prudent to have all your wealth in Canadian dollars. Go for international mutual funds, foreign-denominated bonds, foreign currency dividend income, and so on.

JUNIOR SENIORS

Lots of people aged 55 to 75 make the same mistake, believing they must be satisfied with low-risk investments, and pension and interest income. Wrong and dangerous.

First, you pay the most tax on pension and interest payments. Second, people in their sixties often fail to budget for the future. After all, you stand a good chance of living another 20 years or more, and a huge risk of running out of money before you pass on. Third, interest rates have declined substantially, so investments such as GICs will only offer less income in the future. Cash them in and find something better. Here's how:

1. **Replace maturing GICs with bonds**—Investments such as mortgage-backed securities are a fine idea. Earn a greater return with less risk, more flexibility, and potential for a capital gain. When your GICs mature, invest some of that capital for far greater returns.

2. **You should be 50% invested for growth**—That means quality stocks and equity-based mutual funds.

3. **Use a systematic withdrawal plan for income**—A great way of removing cash from a mutual fund on a regular basis, and pay substantially less tax than you would get on GIC or pension income. Long-term performance is far superior to any return on fixed-income.

For example, a $100,000 investment in Trimark's Canadian-dollar fund in 1981 would have given you a $10,000 annual income and be worth about $500,000 today. Or $100,000 invested in Fidelity Growth America in 1990 would have paid the same and be worth today more than $300,000. Money at your disposal and your capital still keeps amassing—all the quality mutual fund firms offer withdrawal plans.

Action Plan Consideration. . .

A systematic withdrawal plan works well when leveraging your home equity. Take out an interest-only loan of $50,000, $100,000 or more against your home. Put the money into a quality mutual fund, and have the fund make monthly payments to cover the loan. Not only will the fund continue to deliver solid returns, but the money it pays to satisfy the loan can be deducted from your income taxes. Your assets grow and taxes decrease.

4. **Don't sit on real estate equity**—Why have tens of thousands of dollars in real estate, earning nothing, when that money could be yielding income? At your age real estate can turn into a trap. If you are over 50, seriously question how much of your wealth you can afford to keep in this non-performing asset.

5. **Get moving on sensible estate planning**—If you do not plan properly, your estate will be decimated by taxes, and your wishes may not be carried out. If you die with real estate, it may saddle your children with a huge tax liability. Dying is a complicated process. You've got to be ready and ask your adviser to put a plan into action.

SENIOR SENIORS

Things finally start to get simpler when you are 75 or older. But with longevity on the rise, people in this age bracket still have a lot of living to do. Bear these points in mind:

1. **Dump the GICs**—Don't lock up money for five-year periods just to get a return of far less than 10%. The yield will be far higher from a government bond (not a savings bond) and you will have liquidity.

2. **Maintain a growth component to your portfolio**—At this age you should still have at least 25% of your assets invested in equity-based mutual funds or quality stocks to give dividend income. The growth will help finance the next decade, and tax implications are far more favourable. And use a systematic withdrawal plan to get regular income from the mutual funds.

3. **Sell real estate now**—Your capital could be earning a lot more in the economy than in your house. The current real estate market is more buoyant than it's been in some time, and you might get a better price today than in a year or two.

4. **Get a financial adviser you trust**—An effective estate plan, along with proper tax planning and investment strategies require the expertise of a trusted adviser.

5. **Go for a cruise**—This is what it's all about. Money is not an object in itself, just a tool to help you accomplish other things. Lighten up! It'll add years to your life.

--●

Chapter 12

Make the most of your severance package

The economy is booming, corporate confidence is soaring, and you've just been let go. Unfortunately, it happens in the best of times. If you're a more senior employee, you could be forced into early retirement. But there are ways to handle these situations and minimize their effects on you, both short and long term.

The best possible place to stash the money you receive on being laid off, fired or just retired, is your RRSP. Termination or severance payments (technically called retiring allowances) can be rolled into an RRSP. If your former employer does this for you, then no tax is withheld.

If you accept a cheque (really bad move) and then put the money in an RRSP, you will lose 30% in taxes—which you can claim back later on your tax return. But you lose precious time in which that sum could have been compounding tax-free in your RRSP. You don't need that hassle right now.

HOW MUCH CAN I ROLL OVER?

As of the 1996 budget, the ability to roll over retiring allowances was eliminated. This was a travesty, especially for those entering the work-force in the past five years. For those with a work history before then, for each year, or part of a year, prior to 1996 that you worked, you are still eligible to put $2,000 into your RRSP. In addition, you can contribute $1,500 for each year prior to 1989 that you were not part of the company's pension plan or deferred profit-sharing plan. The best part? This amount does not count towards your personal contribution limits.

For example, if you had worked for 25 years and were laid off in 2000, and were part of a company pension plan, you could put $42,000 into your RRSP (that's $2,000 for the 21 years worked prior to 1996).

If you worked the same length of time, and never contributed to a company pension plan, the eligible RRSP contribution would be $63,000 (you add $1,500 for each of the 14 years worked prior to 1989 to the $2,000 a year for the 21 years worked prior to 1996).

Now with 1996 as the cut-off date, you will not build up any additional rollover amount, but you will not (for now, at least) lose the amount you earned prior to that. For people just entering the workforce, of course, it means that they will never be able to take advantage of a tax-free retiring allowance.

STAYING AFLOAT

Everyone has financial commitments. Minimize these until a new work situation arises, and you will not regret the sacrifice made for a more comfortable retirement. But life doesn't always go according to plan, and withdrawals are necessary. Need extra cash? You can access up to $5,000 from your RRSP and pay only 10% in tax. Remove $5,000 to $15,000, and the rate increases to 20%. Corresponding rates in Quebec are 21% and 30%. RRSP withdrawals are treated as another form of income—your bank, credit union, trust company or broker is required to withhold some of your withdrawal and send it to Ottawa.

Your financial adviser can provide immeasurable assistance to help you through this tumultuous time. Here are a few things to consider:

- Because the tax rate rises with the amount withdrawn, withdraw money in smaller amounts.
- Check on what limits your financial institution might have to discourage small RRSP withdrawals.
- Claim any tax withheld on your income tax return.

SOME GOOD NEWS

In the 1997 budget, the feds introduced the opportunity for you to recover lost RRSP contribution room if you were in a company pension plan and subject to the pension adjustment calculation. That means that you can roll over your lump-sum pension payout into your RRSP (again, don't take a cheque, just get it transferred), and the lost RRSP room will be restored, minus the amount of the lump sum. This is all well and fine, but if you've just lost your job, there's not much chance that you'll have the money to fill up that space right away. Be sure to use up that room though, when you're back on your feet.

TAKE THE MONEY AND RUN

If you're laid off and offered a right of recall or a severance package—which is the best way to go? Every case is different. If it's a situation where seasonal layoffs are the norm, nine times out of 10, you're better off accepting the package. This may be the only time in your working life when you get a nice lump sum to leverage up retirement assets.

You may be offered to take over your accumulated pension contributions instead of leaving them where they are. Take it. You and your adviser can probably make them grow a lot faster. The decisions you make, of course, depend on your current financial status, monthly spending requirements, future prospects, and a discussion with your spouse and financial adviser.

HERE ARE SOME VALUABLE TIPS TO REMEMBER:

- Ensure that you get all that's coming. Any part of a year—even one day—can qualify for a full year's amount.
- Part-time or seasonal work qualifies, as do co-op job placements and internships.
- Carefully review your employment record before agreeing to a settlement package.
- Ask your employer to put the money directly into an RRSP for you.
- If you accept the severance package, tax will be withheld. But depending on how much of it you then put into an RRSP, you can claim some or all of it back.
- If the amount you are rolling over is huge, you may be nailed by the alternative minimum tax. It may be wise to check whether you can take the package over a couple of tax years.
- Self-employed? Then you have also built up eligible retirement allowance room over the years, and can roll over cash into your RRSP. Self-employed professionals who employ their spouses can give them a one-time retirement allowance payment when the business is being wound down.

- Remember: the retiring allowance RRSP rollover can go into your RRSP in the year it's received, or you can wait and do it in the first 60 days of the next year—depending on what's best for your tax profile.
- Finally, when you have lost your job and are offered a package, it is sometimes tempting to keep a portion in cash, instead of putting it in the RRSP. Bad idea. You will lose up to one-third of it in tax. Better to put it in the plan with no tax deducted, and then withdraw what you need in small amounts ($5,000 or less). That way the withholding tax is only 10%.

Confide in your financial adviser. If you suspect that you could lose your job, or have received notice, your adviser is best prepared to handle your severance and provide you with a plan on managing your period of unemployment. On top of that, good luck.

Chapter 13

What will the government try next?

Many Canadians share the suspicion that there's a war on wealth in this country. And how can you blame them? Our top tax rate is 15% higher than in the United States.

Middle-aged, middle-class people probably have the most to lose over the next two decades. Today's retirees and the near-retired can count on government pension benefits while the younger generations, the most financially literate ever, have four decades to prepare.

FIVE TAX THREATS YOU NEED TO KNOW ABOUT

The threat of any future tax increases does not diminish the importance of RRSPs. Ottawa will tinker with the rules, but I cannot foresee a major attack. But there are threats. Here are the Big Five:

1. YOUR ABILITY TO CATCH UP ON MISSED CONTRIBUTIONS COULD END

It's only a matter of time before the government ends this benefit. Canadians have missed making over $200 billion in contributions. If they did, the government's books would easily plunge into the red from all those rebate cheques. Do not be surprised when the carry-forward provision is altered—either killed outright, returned to pre-1991 rules (make your annual contribution or lose it), or changed to allow a carry-forward for a defined number of years.

Action Plan Requirement...

Use your carry-forward today. Lack the cash? Borrow it. If you have other assets, make a contribution in kind. Any delay is a gamble you need not take.

---

2. RRSP CONTRIBUTIONS COULD BECOME TAX CREDITS, NOT DEDUCTIONS

This would be sneaky—meaning it's not above any government. Today you are allowed to deduct the whole amount of your RRSP contribution from your taxable income. That directly reduces the amount of tax you pay—the more money you make, the more tax you save.

People in the top tax bracket receive 53 cents on every dollar contributed to their RRSP, compared with 25 cents on the dollar for people earning less than $30,000.

If the contribution was treated as a credit, the refund for lower-income earners would remain about the same, but it would tumble for those making more. Those in the top tax bracket would see that 53-cent break dwindle to about 30 cents. An attempt to go this route was thwarted when Bill C-364 bit the dirt. That doesn't mean we've seen the end of this meddling. Be ready to howl if this is revived.

3. RRSP ASSETS COULD BE DIRECTLY TAXED

This was already suggested by Jim Peterson, when he was chairman of the House of Commons finance committee—a 1% annual tax on RRSPs worth more than $500,000. To his credit, Finance Minister Paul Martin didn't go for it. It has political curb appeal, because half a million sounds like a lot and 1% sounds like a very small tax. But the implications are horrific. Such a tax would:

- Seriously compromise the whole intent of the system
- Erode investor confidence
- Rattle financial markets
- Break faith with taxpayers
- Signal that the government cannot be trusted with long-term fiscal and social policy

However, that is no reason it couldn't happen. But even such a backward, myopic move would not overcome the advantages of contributing heavily to an RRSP.

4. CONTRIBUTION LEVELS COULD BE SLASHED AGAIN

The old rules said we should be at the annual $15,500 level by now. But here we are, frozen at $13,500. Today's rules say the limit will be raised in 2003, and eventually indexed to inflation. Only a tiny percentage of Canadians actually qualify to make the top contribution, so dropping it would not have major consequences except to send out the desired political signal that rich layabouts will pay more.

5. THE TIME YOU HAVE TO SAVE COULD BE CUT

It's already started. The 1996 budget reduced by two years the age at which you can no longer contribute to your RRSP. It removed from everyone the potential to shelter from tax tens of thousands of dollars. It shaved 24 months off the time you could have added assets to your plan. And it accelerated the date at which you must start collapsing your savings. And it could drop again. Get ready to howl, part two.

IN CONCLUSION...

Let me make it clear: these are just possibilities. There is no hard evidence that any of these threats will come to pass, but then, anything is possible with governments. Ironically, one of the most foresightful things the government can do is to encourage more private savings for financial independence. It's the best way of dealing with the coming retirement crisis, and the best tool for that is the RRSP.

Let those in power know your concerns. It helped waylay the Seniors Benefit. So nothing is impossible. Here's your MP's address: House of Commons, Ottawa, ON K1A 0A6. You don't even need a stamp.

Chapter 14

Why everybody
needs an adviser

While I hope this book has expanded your knowledge of the investment choices available, it is no substitute for a trusted adviser who knows you and your goals. Most Canadians are gambling horribly with their financial futures because they entrust their money entirely to rank amateurs with no formal training who devote about two hours a year to the job and refuse to consider any research or investment information that isn't free. That's right—they do their own financial planning. Huge mistake. Consider this:

- Six in ten Canadians believe they won't have $250,000 net worth on the day they retire, according to a Gallup poll. Even with public pensions, these folks will see a drastic drop in their standard of living during retirement.
- Record numbers of people have been going bankrupt.
- The national savings rate hit its lowest point ever in 1998.
- Household debt levels continue to climb.
- Most Canadians have too much net worth locked up in one type of asset—residential real estate.
- Two-thirds of Canadians have never made an RRSP contribution.
- Collectively we are more than $200 billion behind in RRSP contributions.
- Most people think Canada Savings Bonds provide an excellent long-term return. Worse still, only 14% of people can identify the best-performing investment class since the Second World War—stocks.
- Crazed investors sold hundreds of millions of dollars worth of mutual funds just days before the last Quebec referendum—just after the TSE 300 had been clobbered and fund values reduced. The day after the referendum, most people bought back the funds—at higher prices.

- People clamour to buy investments at their highest value and then dump them when they fall. Remember the folks lined up to buy gold at $1,000 an ounce? What's it worth today? How about those who bought $1-million homes north of Toronto in 1989? Not long after, half that street was for sale at $500,000 a house. And recall how many investors bailed after Black Monday, 1987? They missed one of the greatest run-ups in stock-market history.
- Millions of Canadians keep billions in GICs, when they could be earning better returns with less risk in other securities, because they've never heard of seg funds, strip bonds or mortgage-backed securities.

BE WARY OF BAD APPLES

News about unethical advisers is never hard to find. In Ontario, a top-producing mutual fund salesman was banned for life after pocketing secret payments and leaving his clients with worthless investments. In Toronto, a financial adviser stole more than $800,000 from the accounts of three elderly clients, including a defenseless woman with Alzheimer's disease. Then there's the recent Royal Trust stock fiasco and the heads that rolled there.

Some advisers turn out to be churners—excessively buying and selling investments just to maximize commissions, at the client's expense. Others are just cheats. Some "top producers" get there, not by making wise investments but rather by racing through legions of clients.

WHAT YOU CAN DO

Approach this exercise with caution, but not with cynicism or skepticism. The key is to find someone with knowledge and integrity. The good news is that there are many to choose from.

Here are my answers to the questions I'm most often asked about finding an adviser you can trust:

How do I know if a planner is qualified?
Are there regulations?
People who sell financial securities must be licensed. But the industry, as a whole, is unregulated, which means finding a good adviser will

take some work on your part. The Canadian Association of Financial Planners has about 1,600 members, accounting for just 20% of all people who call themselves planners. There are currently no national standards, but here are a few designations you may encounter:

- "Registered Financial Planner," or RFP—designation of Canadian Association of Financial Planners
- "Chartered Financial Planner," or CHFP, designates someone who has completed the correspondence course of the Canadian Association of Insurance and Financial Advisers (CAIFA)
- "Chartered Life Underwriter," or CLU—the stamp of approval from CAIFA

To further confuse things, the Canadian Association of Financial Planners and the Life Underwriters have teamed up to create the Financial Planners Standards Council of Canada (FPSCC), which promotes yet another designation, the "Certified Financial Planner," or CFP.

It looks as though this last one is quickly becoming the industry norm, since that term is already recognized in the United States and some other countries.

Meanwhile, the people who train bankers and stockbrokers pulled out of the FPSCC in 1998. So, here are some other designations to look for:

- "Certified Investment Manager," or CIM—sanctioned by the Canadian Securities Institute
- "Personal Financial Planner," or PFP, and "Specialist in Financial Counselling," or SFC—designations of the Institute of Canadian Bankers

Confusing? Yes. So just ask the advisers you are interviewing for a summary of education, special training, experience and, of course, references.

What does good advice cost?

Most people think a financial planner will charge a huge amount of money. Usually, however, that's not the case. Most work for you for free, usually paid through commissions by the mutual fund company, bond issuer or the insurance company when you add an investment to your portfolio. You can hire an adviser who is fee-only and does not arrange for any investments to be made. That will cost you up to

$2,000 for a complete financial plan, with hourly consultation fees ranging from $50 to $250, with most in the $100 area. Then you still need someone to implement the plan, and purchase the securities.

For the vast majority of people who have under $1 million in liquid assets, an adviser who is remunerated through commissions is just fine.

What can you expect? For starters, a free 60- to 90-minute consultation. From there, the adviser prepares an analysis of your assets and drafts a financial plan and recommendations. Typically, it costs you nothing. So you have no excuse for not getting a valuable second opinion on how you're doing.

Eight Common Investor Mistakes an Adviser Can Help You Avoid

- Waiting for the "best" time to invest, or never investing
- Buying at a high price, selling at a low one
- Buying yesterday's hot investment
- Choosing investments not suited to individual goals or time horizons
- Failing to diversify
- Reacting to short-term events rather than long-term trends
- Basing investment decisions on fees and sales charges
- Basing investment decisions on emotions rather than facts

Source: Mutual Fund Forum

Where do I start?

Word-of-mouth references are valuable because you can get a feel for an adviser's track record from somebody you know. You can respond to ads published in the financial section of your local newspaper, or in the *Financial Post.*

Better yet, attend a few financial seminars. The financial planners hosting them invariably offer any attendees a free consultation. But beware: not all seminars are what they appear. Some are come-ons for expensive and needless courses on no-money-down real estate or sure-thing business opportunities. So, if you attend one, leave your cheque-book at home.

Listen and you can quickly determine if it's a sales pitch—with one or two specific investment products being hyped—or the introduction of a useful service and an adviser who sounds promising.

What questions should I ask?

During that first meeting, the adviser will ask for a lot of information on your income, assets, taxes, family situation and goals. In return, you should be prepared to dig up as much information as possible on him or her. Be tough. Be frank. Be candid. To make this grilling easier, here's a list of questions that American investors are urged to ask of a potential planner, as published in the *Wall Street Journal*:

Things You Should Ask Advisers During Interviews

- What is your area of expertise?
- What is your approach to saving and investing?
- Will you provide an individualized financial plan?
- What kinds of communications are sent on an ongoing basis (account statements, newsletters)?
- How often will you review my portfolio?
- How are you compensated for the service you provide?
- How are fees calculated?
- On average, how much can I expect to pay for your service?
- What do I receive in return for that fee?
- What, if anything, do you expect of me during our relationship?

Should I ask for references?

Absolutely. In fact, this is the most important information to ask for. A good adviser has nothing to hide. In fact, a good adviser will be proud of his or her clients' success, and will want to share it with you.

So ask for a list of 10 or 12 people whom the adviser has worked with. Then call and ask for a candid appraisal of the planner's effectiveness. Has the adviser:

- Reduced their tax bill?
- Increased their net worth?
- Diversified their investments? Plus. . .
- What overall rate of return are they getting on their portfolios?

Source: David Brown, Toronto Star

- How often do they hear from the adviser?
- Are they kept fully informed?
- Are they concerned about excessive trading in their accounts?
- Are they related to the adviser? (It does happen!)

What level of service should I expect?

Several initial meetings to approve an investment and tax strategy, followed by regular updates—perhaps quarterly. Your portfolio should be reviewed several times a year, or as changing conditions dictate.

You should receive a regular statement—monthly is best—and it should break down all transactions, providing rates of return and securities held along with weightings by asset class (for example, 41% mutual funds, 32% fixed income, 27% equities).

Many good advisers provide clients with newsletters, access to investment research or client appreciation nights where investment professionals come to speak. The most important thing to expect is a comfortable working relationship with somebody you trust.

How can I tell if it's not working?

A telltale sign that you're working with the wrong person is churning. That's when the adviser is buying and selling a lot of mutual fund units or stocks for no good reason other than to earn more in commissions.

What's the difference between a planner, a broker and a counsellor?

Many planners work for companies that offer a full range of financial products, including strip bonds, stocks, mutual funds, GICs and more. These planners usually earn their living through commissions paid by fund and other companies.

A broker is licensed to sell any financial product and must have completed the Canadian Securities Course. He or she will work for a brokerage company regulated by the Investment Dealers Association of Canada. A broker also earns money through commissions on every transaction.

An investment counsellor is paid through fees that can take the form of an annual payment or a percentage of the total portfolio under management. Usually counsellors are the preserve of those with more than $500,000 in investment assets.

How do I know if an adviser is full-service?

Ask. Some planners only sell mutual funds, so obviously they will not be able to give your portfolio the required balance and diversity. You want an adviser who will look at your total financial picture—real estate, insurance, estate, tax and investment plans.

What about discount brokers?

These are no-frills operations that allow you to buy stocks, bonds or funds at a vastly cheaper commission cost than with a full-service broker or planner. Examples are T-D's impressive Green Line operation and the Royal Bank's Action Direct. Discount brokers are innovative and cutting-edge in terms of the latest investor technology. Canada Trust, Action Direct and Green Line all offer real-time trading via personal computer.

The downside is the same as with no-load mutual funds—no help. The people on the phone are order-takers, not experienced investment advisers. But if you know what you want, and are determined to save money on commissions, then go for it, increased risk and all.

Should I go with a small company or a big one?

There is no right answer to this question, because it is the individual adviser who really matters. With a small office or firm you stand a better chance of receiving personal attention. But with a large firm, access to research and a full range of investment options are pluses. My personal recommendation would be to find a small office of a big company.

Always remember: a good financial adviser is more interested in a long-term relationship than in making quick commissions. As your wealth grows, so does the adviser's compensation—so over a 15- or 20-year time line, your financial well-being is your adviser's main concern.

Should I give over all my money?

Probably not—at least not at first. You must build a relationship and see your adviser at work. So, don't write a cheque representing your life savings right off the bat. But, by the same token, don't hand over $5,000 and expect to see dramatic results in a few weeks

Once you feel comfortable with the advice you are getting, it makes sense to consolidate your portfolio with one person.

Here's how to reach me

Attend one of my financial seminars and meet some planners. Follow it up with a consultation, and make up your own mind. If you'd like the names of advisers who I might know in your area, send me a fax or an e-mail. Last year, more than 8,000 people did! You can access my current seminar schedule through my Internet website. I can be reached:

- By phone: (416) 489-2188
- By fax: (416) 489-2189
- By e-mail: garth@garth.ca
- On the World Wide Web: http://www.garth.ca
- By mail: Garth Turner
  Suite 310, 1670 Bayview Ave.,
  Toronto, ON M4G 3C2

The Turner Report

YOUR BEST DEFENCE: KNOWLEDGE

The Turner Report is a monthly newsletter that will give you an update of this book, the best investment advice I can find, plus answers to the questions that must be answered. It is published 10 times a year and its intention is clear: present up-to-the-minute methods for reducing tax exposure, and investment opportunities that make sense. It covers mutual funds, strip bonds, seg funds, real estate, precious metals, stocks, oil and gas and all aspects of personal finance.

AN AFFORDABLE NEWSLETTER OF TAX AND INVESTMENT STRATEGIES

The Turner Report does not suffer the long lead times that books demand, nor is it another Bay Street publication written by a committee. It has nothing to sell. Instead, it's the living extension of this book, my financial guide for baby boomers, *2020: New Rules for the New Age*, *The Defence*, *2015: After the Boom*, and *The Strategy*. It is as timely and inexpensive as I can possibly make it.

In every issue:

- A national panel of top financial advisers provides expert advice to individual subscribers.
- Product Showcase offers an inside look at some of the hottest funds available, and their performance.
- Features on the best tax and investment strategies.
- My personal analysis of current economic and market events, and predictions of where we're headed.
- Special offers to subscribers, including advance ordering of my books before they are available anywhere else.

The cost? Less than $5 an issue. I'll send you the first issue as a gift for subscribing. Not satisfied? Return it for a full refund. No risk.

Many good investment newsletters are currently available. But if I thought any one of them was adequate for aggressive middle-class Canadians, aged 30 to 65, who are determined to succeed, then I would simply recommend one of them instead of writing my own.

But to date, I haven't found one that combines tax and investment strategies in the big-picture context of where the economy is headed or what impact demographics will have. And now, more than ever, the difference between financial independence and dependence has come down to one thing, and one thing only: knowledge.

Clip or photocopy this coupon, and send it to me at: Suite 310, 1670 Bayview Ave., Toronto, Ont. M4G 3C2 or, subscribe online at www.garth.ca.

Subscribe now, and get your first issue FREE

A special offer for new subscribers: The first issue will be sent to you without charge. Your subscription will start with the next issue. If you are not pleased, return it for a full refund.

❑ By E-mail: $40 a year
❑ By Lettermail: $49 a year
❑ By Fax: $59 a year

Name: _____

Address: _____ Apt.: _____

City: _____ Prov.: _____ Code: _____

Phone: Home ( ) _____ Business ( ) _____

E-mail: _____ Fax: ( ) _____

❑ Enclosed is: My cheque payable to *The Turner Report*

❑ Bill my **Visa** # __ __ __ __ / __ __ __ __ / __ __ __ __ / __ __ __ __

❑ Bill my **MasterCard** # __ __ __ __ / __ __ __ __ / __ __ __ __ / __ __ __ __

Mail to:
The Turner Report
310—1670 Bayview Ave.,
Toronto M4G 3C2

Fax:
(416) 489-2189

E-mail:
Garth@garth.ca   Prices valid in Canada only.

Expiry __ __ / __ __

Appendix

2000 PERSONAL INCOME TAX RATES (%)
Combined federal and provincial
Source: Grant Thornton

2000

taxable income	$6,750–28,000	$28,000–36,000	$36,000–40,000	$40,000–60,000	$60,000–64,000	$64,000 & over
British Columbia						
Salary	25.4	25.4/37.4	37.4	37.4/47.7	47.7	47.7/51.3
Interest	26.4	37.4	37.4	37.4/47.7	47.7	47.7/51.3
Dividends	7.1	21.8	21.8	21.8/29.3	29.3	29.3/32.2
Alberta						
Salary	25.0	25.0/36.5	36.5	36.5/37.7	37.7/43.1	43.7
Interest	25.8	36.5	36.5	36.5/42.2	42.2	42.2/43.7
Dividends	7.4	21.6	21.6	21.6/28.8	28.8	28.8
Saskatchewan						
Salary	27.6	27.6/39.9	39.9	39.9/48.2	48.2/48.3	48.3/49.7
Interest	29.1	39.9	39.9	39.9/48.2	48.2	48.2/49.7
Dividends	10.0	26.3	24.3	24.3/32.7	32.7	32.7/33.7
Manitoba						
Salary	27.9	27.9/41.2	41.2	41.2/46.6	46.6	46.6/49.7
Interest	28.4	41.2	41.2	41.2/46.6	46.6	46.6/48.1
Dividends	9.6	27.0	27.0	27.0/33.8	33.8	33.8
Ontario						
Salary	23.4	23.4/34.6	34.6	34.6/43.9	43.9/46.4	46.4/47.9
Interest	27.0	34.6	34.6	34.6/44.0	44.0	44.0/47.9
Dividends	7.3	20.2	20.2	20.2/27.1	27.1	27.1/31.3
New Brunswick						
Salary	28.0	28.0/40.2	40.2	40.2/46.0	46.0	46.0/48.8
Interest	28.4	39.6	39.6	39.6/45.9	45.9	45.9/48.8
Dividends	7.7	23.1	23.1	23.1	23.1	23.1/32.0

2000 PERSONAL INCOME TAX RATES (%) continued
Combined federal and provincial

Nova Scotia

Salary	26.8/27.8	27.8/40.0	40.0	40.0/45.6	45.6/45.7	45.7/48.8
Interest	27.6	39.4	39.4	39.4/45.6	45.6	45.6/48.8
Dividends	7.5	23.0	23.0	23.0	23.0	23.0/32.9

Prince Edward Island

Salary	26.8	26.8/39.4	39.4	39.4/47.3	47.3	47.3/48.8
Interest	27.6	39.4	39.4	39.4/47.3	47.3	47.3/48.8
Dividends	7.5	23.0	23.0	23.0/23.8	23.8	23.8/32.9

Newfoundland

Salary	24.0	37.3	37.3	37.3/43.2	43.2	45.4
Interest	26.0	37.3	37.3	37.3/43.2	43.2	45.4
Dividends	7.0	21.7	21.7	21.7/29.2	29.2	29.2/29.7

Yukon

Salary	24.0	37.3	37.3	37.3/43.2	43.2	45.4
Interest	26.0	37.3	37.3	37.3/43.2	43.2	45.4
Dividends	7.0	21.7	21.7	21.7/29.2	29.2	29.2/29.7

Northwest Territories

Salary	23.2	35.3	35.3	35.3/41.3	41.3	41.3/43.5
Interest	25.2	35.3	35.3	35.3/41.3	41.3	41.3/43.5
Dividends	6.8	20.2	20.2	20.2/28.4	28.4	28.4

Combined federal and provincial rates for Quebec

On Salary

Taxable Income	Rate
$20,000–24,000	33.2
$24,001–28,000	33.2/36.7
$28,001–50,000	36.7/43.4
$50,001–58,000	43.4/45.9
$58,001–60,000	45.9/49.2
$60,001–70,000	49.2/49.4
$70,001 and over	49.4/50.7

On Investment Income

Taxable Income	Interest	Dividends	Capital Gains
$20,000–24,000	33.2	19.4	27.1
$24,001–28,000	33.2/36.7	26.8	28.6
$28,001–40,000	36.7/43.4	26.8	34.5
$40,001–50,000	43.4	26.8	35.3
$50,001–60,000	43.4/49.2	26.8/29.9	36.1
$60,001 and over	49.2/50.7	29.9/35.0	39.5

Index